The Illustrated Book of Housebuilding and Carpentry

The Illustrated Book of Housebuilding and Carpentry

2 Volumes in 1

Originally published under the titles:
Illustrated Housebuilding
and
Illustrated Interior Carpentry

Written and illustrated by
Graham Blackburn

GRAMERCY PUBLISHING COMPANY
New York

Even a work of fiction is the result of an author's experience, and as such owes a large debt for its creation to all the other people who have played a part in the author's life. A book of facts is even more the result of other people, for it is an objective account of their discoveries and actions in thier lives and on their surroundings rather than a subjective account of their influence upon the author's personal story. Therefore, it would be most ungrateful and unrealistic were I not to mention the people in my life who have helped to make this book possible.

I would like to thank my father, who taught me the right attitude; Harris, who taught me respect for the craft; R. J. Puttick, who taught me that form was as important as function, and that we would all build houses one day; Lubinsky, who brought me to the right place; Holly & Teddy, who provided me with the opportunity; Heide and Oliver, who demonstrated the necessity and rewards of necessities; Elaine, who proved them; and lastly, all the craftsmen of Woodstock who offered criticism, advice, and encouragement.

SPECIAL THANKS TO

My favorite editor, Evelyn Gendel, who helped conceive this book; my favorite publisher; Peter Mayer, who gave me my start and thus made all my books possible; my best friends, Barry Cahn, John Holbrook, and Paul Potash, who at various times looked after me during the writing of this book; Lynda Redfield, Denis Dehr, and Tom Laine, who in different ways provided the high points of the year; Nick Jameson for being so generous with his Steinway; Mara Lepmarris for being so special; Elaine Louie, Thomas Holman, Douglas Holman, and Geoffrey Stephenson for making life fun; Sandra Shaw for being Maid Marian all the way from Woodstock to Houston and Appaloosa all the way from Houston to Los Angeles; Carol Glenn for being my favorite photographer; Thomas Gayton for enlivening Neptune Beach; Carolyn, Rebecca, and Sabrina Berliner for being my favorite family in Hollywood; and Tina Whitney Firestone, without whom my (and many other people's) life would be much duller.

Originally published in two separate volumes by the Overlook Press, Inc.
Illustrated Housebuilding, copyright © 1974 by G. J. Blackburn
Illustrated Interior Carpentry, copyright © 1978 by G. J. Blackburn
All rights reserved.

This 1990 edition is published by Gramercy Publishing Company, distributed by Outlet Book Company, Inc., a Random House Company, 225 Park Avenue South, New York, New York 10003, by arrangement with The Overlook Press, Inc.

Printed and bound in the United States of America

Library of Congress Cataloging-in-Publication Data

Blackburn, Graham, 1940-
    Illustrated book of housebuilding and carpentry / by Graham
Blackburn.
        p.   cm.
    "2 volumes in 1."
    Includes bibliographical references.
    ISBN 0-517-03311-9
    1. Wooden-frame houses—Design and construction—Amateurs'
manuals.   2. Carpentry—Amateurs' manuals.   I. Title.
TH4818.W6B54   1990
694—dc20   90-35296
                                                                                     CIP

ISBN 0-517-03311-9

8 7 6 5 4 3 2 1

Illustrated Housebuilding

with respect to all the old Carpenters
who originally figured it out

CONTENTS

More than a century has elapsed since an ingenious and useful work

on the Arts connected with Building was published under the title of

MECHANICAL EXERCISES by the celebrated Joseph Moxon:

that it was both useful and popular the various editions testify, and at

this time it is become scarce and rarely to be met with. It can be

no disparagement to its ingenious author, to say, that the progress

of science, and the changes in matters of art have rendered the

work obsolete . . .

Peter Nicholson, 1812

from the Preface to Peter Nicholson's book,

Mechanical Exercises; or, the
Elements and Practice of
Carpentry, Joinery, Bricklaying, etc.

INTRODUCTION

Gone are the days when trades were learned with seven year apprenticeships, which like everything else, is partly good and partly bad. In this case good because it gives us more leisure, but bad because while techniques and materials may have become more sophisticated the level of enduring craftsmanship has dropped. So while I have tried to explain the standards and techniques for building a substantial, well-built house, it should be realized that these are no longer the only criteria. Many houses are built primarily for immediate profit, and so economy and speed are often more important considerations than durability or beauty.

Illustrated Housebuilding presents essentially the method used in building the standard frame house, a direct descendant of early colonial and pioneer houses, which were developed from European models adapted to a new environment and different requirements. However, any step, once understood in itself and in relation to the other steps involved, may be modified in an almost limitless number of ways.

AMERICAN COLONIAL HOUSE

TYPICAL FLOOR PLANS

The order of steps may be changed to a certain extent. The dimensions, while basically a function of such things as standard lumber sizes and building codes, may be changed to suit your own taste and convenience. The point is that while the method may be basically similar, the designs may vary considerably. It is only necessary to look around at other buildings to see that while the majority are all constructed on the same principles as explained in this book, hardly any two look exactly alike.

It is important to remember that while each chapter is complete in itself, to be completely understood it should be read in context with the rest of the book. Read the whole book first before attempting any one stage and you will have a better idea of what you are doing, and why.

The final point I would like to make is that this is a basic method, and not a definitive encyclopedia of all possible ways of housebuilding. Therefore, at the end of each chapter there is a relevant bibliography containing sources for more specialized information for each stage of construction.

CHAPTER ONE. Site and Foundation

THE SITE

The very first thing to think about once you have decided to build a house is *where* to build it. Here is a list of things to consider:

1. The Axis of the House.
2. The Slope of the Land.
3. Drainage.
4. Water Supply.
5. Access.
6. View.
7. Internal Functions.
8. Privacy & Neighbors.

1. The Axis of the House.

You will want to consider how the house lies—that is, which way is front and back, and which are the sides, and how the whole thing sits in relation to the sun. If you build in the Northern Hemisphere remember that the part of the house facing South gets sun all day long. If you like being awakened by the early morning sun, build the bedrooms on the Eastern side. North light is best for studios. If you live in a snow area, it helps to have the front door on the Southern side—the snow melts quickest here.

2. The Slope of the Land.

Unless your land is perfectly flat the slope will affect things. If it is very steep there will be more foundation work and you will have to think carefully about floor levels and entrances—but you will also have greater opportunity for balconies.

foundation →

House A has a foundation many times deeper than house B, but could have a dramatic balcony on the high side. House B may be entered easily from any side.

3. Drainage.

Try and choose a dry spot to build on. It will make the foundation work much easier if you do not have to excavate in a marsh! A dry, gently sloping area will be better for your sewage system than a flat, boggy area. Remember also, if you are inspecting the land in the summer, that many dry stream beds become raging torrents during the rest of the year.

4. Water Supply.

Locating the house downhill from an available water supply such as a spring or a stream can save a lot of money on wells, pumps and pressure tanks. But be sure the spring or stream will not dry up if it doesn't rain for a while!

Gravity-Fed Water Supply

5. Access.

Remember that no matter how well the location of the site fulfills all other conditions you must be able to get to it. It is, of course, possible to carry everything in by hand if you decide to build deep in the woods or high on a mountain, but it is much easier if there is easy access to the road. It helps a lot if trucks can deliver material right to the site. If you live in a snow area remember that the cost of having your driveway plowed in the winter increases with its length—the driveway's and the winter's. Remember too that it is hard to drive (and walk, especially with groceries) up a long, steep driveway covered with ice in mid-winter.

Unless you aim to be primitive or maintain your own generator bear in mind that it is expensive to bring in electricity. Utility companies require poles for overhead power lines every 150 feet or so, and it is becoming mandatory in more and more areas to install underground "service" or power lines, which is even more expensive—although it looks better, lasts longer and is not subject to damage by wind, snow or ice. So the nearer you can build to an existing power supply the cheaper it will be.

6. View.

In the past, people who built houses in the country generally spent most of their time out of doors and consequently were not concerned with "bringing the outdoors indoors." They also did not have insulated windows and so the fewer they had, and the smaller they were, the easier it was to keep the house warm. Nowadays, however, this is not the case, and a good view can add much pleasure, as well as value, to a house.

7. Internal Functions.

How you plan to use the house can affect where you locate it and how you design the inside. For instance, workshops are more conveniently situated at ground level where deliveries may be made easily. Bedrooms are better on the quiet side of the house. The view may be nicest from the living area, and so on.

8. Privacy and Neighbors.

If you enjoy privacy don't build near your property boundaries unless you are certain the adjacent land is not going to be developed. Remember too that deciduous trees lose their leaves in winter and you may then discover neighbors who were invisible all summer.

IMPORTANT! Check out the legal requirements explained in the Appendix—these may also affect where you build.

THE FOUNDATION

Many early American buildings were constructed almost without foundations. One or two courses (layers, in masonry) of rough stone, picked from the fields, were simply laid on top of the ground, and this formed the base for the whole building. No excavation was attempted and the only reason for the stones was to prevent the bottom of the walls from rotting on the wet ground. Over the years, however, the ground settles and the frost and ice work on the stones until the sills (the bottom beams of the house) do come in contact with the ground where they rot out and cause the building to fall over or collapse. There are a few of these buildings, mostly barns, still standing, but for all practical purposes there are really only two ways of starting a house. One is to build a house on **PIERS**, and the other is to build a house on a **FULL FOUNDATION**.

A Barn built right on the Ground.

End View of Frame of Barn.

PIERS are simply legs stuck in the ground on which the house stands!

A House built on Piers.

Piers may be made of laid up stone, concrete block, reinforced concrete, metal or just plain timber posts. Locust posts * are the best if wood is used; they are extremely resistant to rot. Piers are good for building in marshy ground, sandy ground or water.

The Florida Indians who live in the Everglades build their houses on piers.

* Posts made from the wood of the Locust tree.

A House with a Full Foundation.

FULL FOUNDATIONS are best; they are not likely to tilt or fall over as piers sometimes do; they provide better insulation for the underside of the house; they provide a protected space for the "works" of a house, i.e., the furnace, the electrical wiring and most of the plumbing; they may be used as garages, extra rooms or simply for storage space; and one last advantage, banks are often more willing to make loans on houses with full foundations.

CONSTRUCTION OF A FULL FOUNDATION

The construction of the foundation may be dealt with in four stages:

1. Locating the Building Lines.
2. Excavating.
3. Making the Footings.
4. Building the Foundation Walls.

1. Locating the Building Lines.

Having chosen the site for the house the exact location of the foundation must now be determined. However, if the ground is not clear you will save much time and expense by cutting down anything which is growing and stacking the resultant brush somewhere neatly away from the site. If there is anything bigger than 3" (inches) in diameter leave about 18" of it standing—it makes it easier for the bulldozer to push out.

There are two lines which must now be determined: the excavation line, and the line marking the exact position of the outside of the foundation walls, sometimes called the "face line".

The excavation line may be shown by pouring garden lime on the ground where the bulldozer is to dig. This line should be about 3' (feet) outside the face line. The face line should be indicated with line (string or twine) stretched taut between "batter boards". A batter board may be made simply by driving two stakes in the ground and nailing a horizontal piece of wood to them on which to tie the line.

using a Plumb Bob to locate face line on ground.

Line marking the exact location of the foundation walls, stretched taut between batter boards at the proposed corners of the building

STAKES 2' high   A Batter Board

Too much care cannot be taken in ensuring that the face line is exactly located. A simple way of checking, for small rectangular buildings, is first to make sure that the opposite sides are equal and then to measure the diagonals. If the diagonals are equal then the corners will be perfect right angles (i.e. 90°), and the building will be "square."

2. Excavating.

You must now hire a man with a bulldozer to excavate the area you have indicated with the lime. Digging it out yourself with pickax, shovel and wheelbarrow is possible, but would take you weeks. (One reason why the old guys sometimes built straight on the ground!)

The bulldozer should excavate the area so that the bottom is as flat and level as possible and at least one foot below the **FROST LINE.**

The **FROST LINE** is the depth to which frost reaches. Below this line the ground, rarely freezing, stays firm and the house will rest securely on this ground. If the house foundations are built above this line, the ground below may freeze and in so doing move and heave, breaking the foundation and making the house unsafe! The NATIONAL BUILDING CODE requires a minimum of 1'-0" (one foot) below Frost Line. Local Building Codes will tell you how deep the frost line is in your area. Should you encounter bedrock—solid rock—before you reach the appropriate depth you may stop there since bedrock will not move no matter how cold it gets. Even if you build where there is no freezing weather you should still be at least 1'-6" below "grade" (ground level) to assure a firm and level base for the house.

3. Making the Footings.

The **FOOTING** is a small but wide concrete platform running around the proposed perimeter of the building on which the foundation wall will rest. It is made at least a third wider than the foundation wall in order to distribute the load to be borne over a wider area and so prevent settling.

The Footing in the Excavation.

The footing is made with concrete which is best delivered to the site ready mixed in a large truck by a firm which specializes in this. Once again, you could mix it yourself but the footings will be much stronger if poured all at the same time, and even for a relatively small house, say 20′ by 30′, the first batch would be "set up" (dry and hard) before you mixed the last batch. Look in the Yellow Pages of the telephone directory under "Concrete-Ready Mixed" to find a supplier. Tell them the size of the house and they will estimate how much concrete you will need. (It is calculated in cubic yards.) Unless *all* parts of the footing are accessible by the truck it will dump the concrete in one place and you will have to have some friends on hand to help spread the concrete around evenly before it becomes too stiff to move. This can be the hardest part of building the whole house, and it is also the most important, being in all senses the "foundation" of everything else. So be ready!

The concrete is poured into a form—a temporary wooden "mold," which is removed after the concrete is hard. Concrete must be protected against quick drying if cracks and structural weaknesses (not always visible) are to be avoided. Leaving the forms on for a few days after the concrete has been poured is generally sufficient protection. Actually the concrete continues "curing" or drying and hardening for many years.

The form for the concrete is easily built; a typical form is shown below.

Make these sides from boards 2″ x 10″, nailed to the stakes.

Make these stakes from wood 2″ x 4″. Drive them firmly into the ground about every 4′. The form must be strong because concrete is very heavy.

Use the longest boards 2″ thick by 10″ wide (commonly referred to as 2″ x 10″ ′s) you can find. Lumberyards usually carry them in 12′, 14′, 16′ and sometimes 18′

lengths. Stand them on edge and nail them firmly to 2′ stakes made from sharpened pieces of 2″ x 4″ lumber.

Assuming you are going to build the foundation wall with concrete blocks 8″ wide, remember that the footing should be at least ⅓ again as wide, so make the two sides of the form about 16″ apart to be safe. Use the plumb bob hanging from the face line, as shown before, to position the forms.

Face line indicates the exact location of the outside of the foundation walls.

Dotted lines mark where the forms for the footing should go.

It is most important to make sure that the forms are PERFECTLY level; otherwise the footings will be sloping and you will have a hard time trying to make the foundation walls level, and in turn, the house itself! The excavator usually has instruments such as transits and Y levels and will have made the bottom of the hole pretty flat, but you must level up the tops of the forms using a long spirit level on the boards. It is also a good idea to stretch a line, tied to the tops of the form, diagonally, from one corner to the other, and hang a line level on it.

A Spirit Level. These come in many lengths; use the longest one you can find—4′ or even 6′.

Both the spirit level and the line level have transparent tubes filled with colored liquid * in which there is a bubble. When the bubble is between the two lines marked on the tube the wood or the line is perfectly level.

* Sometimes clear.

A Line Level.

When the forms have been built and you are satisfied they are stout, properly positioned and level, you will be ready for the concrete. Hope for a dry, warm day and arm yourself with a hoe—an ordinary garden hoe will do—and a square spade, with which to pull the concrete into place. When the concrete is poured from the truck you must make sure every part of the form is filled. Spading the concrete will eliminate any air pockets and help it settle flat. To get the top of the concrete—between the two sides of the form—level and smooth, use a "strike board", which may be any straight piece of wood longer than the footings are wide. Move the strike board quickly from side to side while at the same time pulling it slowly along the top of the form.

How to use a Strike Board
to level the Footings.

Wash the spade and hoe as soon as you have finished using them or the concrete will dry on them and you will have a hard time chipping it off later. As soon as you can walk on the footings without leaving footprints—within a day or so, depending on the dampness of the weather—you are ready to start on the walls. However, it is a good idea to leave the forms on until the walls are up.

4. Building the Foundation Walls.

Local Building Codes may specify the thickness required for Foundation Walls, but generally, for a small house where the foundation is not going to be much over 6′ deep you may use concrete blocks of the 8″ x 8″ x 16″ size. They actually measure slightly less, as shown below.

A standard 3 core (hole) 8″ x 8″ x 16″ block.

A 2 core corner block. The measurements are the same. Most blocks are now made with 2 cores instead of 3.

Concrete blocks are made from Portland Cement, water and various aggregates such as sand, gravel, cinders or processed slag. They come in many different shapes and sizes, but you will only need the two kinds shown. Whether you get the 2 core type or the 3 core type makes little difference, but you should notice that the "webs" are thicker on one side than the other, and in laying, it is the thick-webbed side which should be up—the better to receive the mortar.

Cross-section of a 3 core block.
(Right way up for laying.)

The blocks are cemented together with mortar, the "recipe" for which is 1 part masonry cement to 3 parts dry sand. Mix the cement and sand thoroughly and then slowly add water until the mix is about the consistency of stiff oatmeal. If you have made it too wet it will run all over the place and you must continue to add commensurate amounts of sand and cement. If you have not added enough water it will be too stiff, and will crumble and not stick to the block.

Cement comes in 94 lb. bags which each contain approximately 1 cubic foot.
Sand is measured by the cubic yard, and must be dry, clean mason's sand.
To estimate what you will need for your foundation use the following table.

For every 100 square feet of wall, using 8″ x 8 ″ x 16″ block	BLOCK	MORTAR	CEMENT	SAND
	110	3¼ cu. ft.	3 bags	¼ cu. yd.

In ordering materials allow at least 10% for waste and remember that a lot depends on how neat and skillful you are.

The depth of the foundation below grade has already been determined by the Frost Line. Bear in mind that the top of the foundation wall should rise two courses or so above grade and you will be able to figure out the area of the wall and the amount of block, sand and cement needed. There is, of course, no reason why you may not make the foundation deeper than the frost line requires if you should need to for any reason—for example if you are planning on installing a furnace which requires more headroom.

The easiest way to make mortar is with a small cement mixer run by a gasoline engine or electricity. It is also possible to do it by hand, although this represents a lot of work even if your foundation is as small as 16′ x 20′, so rent or borrow one if at all possible. The local lumberyard will tell you where. You must have water now too, so if there is no stream or neighbor nearby, and you haven't yet had a well dug, you must bring it in yourself—by hand, truck or whatever.

Order the materials from either the lumberyard or the Ready-Mix Concrete firm and try and have the block delivered in the middle of the site so that it will be equidistant from all points where it will be needed and you will save yourself a lot of heavy carrying. Have the sand and cement left outside the foundation area near the water supply. Make some provision for keeping the cement dry in case of rain, such as covering it with plastic which may be bought in long rolls from lumberyards. Sweep the top of the footings clean and you are ready to begin laying block.

LAYING THE BLOCK

1. Method

1. Use the plumb bob to locate the corners of the foundation wall on the footing.

2. Lay out the block around the entire foundation (without mortar), shifting the blocks one way or another so that they will fit between the corners you have marked, leaving about ⅜″ to ½″ for the mortar between each block. This is called CHASING THE BOND. When you have got everything to fit make chalk marks on the footing where the joints come.

The right tool for cutting block is the Brick Hammer, but the Carpenter's Hammer may be substituted.

Carpenter's Hammer.

Brick Hammer.

It rarely works out exactly, so you will probably have to cut a block or two to get everything to fit. The block may be easily cut to size by first carefully scoring it all around with the blade of your hammer where you want to cut it, and then hitting the part to be broken off sharply with the face of the hammer.

1. Mark cut.   2. Score cut with blade   3. Knock off unwanted
                         of hammer.   part of block.

How to Cut Block.

3. First, lay up three or four courses at the corners. Use plumb bob and level to keep corners straight and plumb.

4. After the corners have been built up, fill in the sides, using the chalk marks to position the blocks. Use cut nails to secure the line as they will not turn in the soft mortar joints. (Also useful are several different patent line-holders available at hardware stores.)

2. Application

The mortar joints should be between ⅜″ and ½″ thick. Sometimes you will have to make them a little thicker or a little thinner in order to have the blocks come out right. The joints should always be staggered—that is, never one joint directly above another. Mortar should be laid only on the outside edges of the block since this method forms an air space in the center which helps to keep the wall dry. Remember to lay the block with the thick webs uppermost.

The only tools you need are a mortar board—somewhere to put the mortar (a wheelbarrow will do, or a flat board on the ground), a pointed trowel with which to apply the mortar, and a mason's level to keep everything straight, plumb and level.

CORNER BLOCK

CUT NAIL

① Apply mortar to both edges of block.

TAUT LINE

FOOTING

BRICKLAYER'S TROWEL

② Stand block on end and apply mortar to two end edges.

③ Pick the block up and shove it firmly against the previous block.

The mortar which is squeezed out between the blocks is cut off with the trowel and placed on the next block, or thrown back on the mortar board. Lay the block so that it just touches the guide line, tap it with the handle of the trowel to sit it straight and check it lengthways, crossways, and diagonally with the level.

check with level

4. Tap block with handle of trowel so that it is both level, and flush with the guide line.

Guide Line.

chalk marks.

Cut off excess mortar with trowel.

Plumb Bobs

A Gun Metal Plumb Bob with a steel point.

Japanned Iron Plumb Bob.

Steel, bored and filled with Mercury. Fitted with braided silk line.

There remain but four more operations before the foundation is complete.

> **1.** Ventilation.   **3.** Anchor Bolts.
> **2.** Provision for Girders.   **4.** Waterproofing.

1. Ventilation.

If the foundation you are building is big enough to stand up in it is called a basement; anything lower is called a crawl space. Basement or crawl space, it must be vented to avoid rot on the bottom of the house. All that needs to be done is to insert an aluminum screened vent in the wall, as high as possible—usually in the penultimate course, at the rate of one for every 50 lineal feet, or a minimum of one in every wall. They measure the same as the face of a block, i.e., 8″ x 16″, and so merely take the place of a whole block.

Use a piece of wood or block here to support the next course until the mortar is dry.

Vents may be installed with regular block as above or with special "vent block" as below.

This sort makes it easier to lay the next course of block. Be careful with the mortar; fill the exposed cores.

2. Provision for Girders.

In any but a *very* small house the joists which support the floor will rest not only on the foundation walls, but on extra supports called girders inside the walls. Whether or not this is necessary belongs to Chapter 2, but in the event it is, provision must be made now, while the walls are being built.

Determine how big the girder is going to be and leave a recessed space big enough to support the end of the girder. Do this by cutting away part of a block (or blocks) before laying them.

See the illustration on the next page.

A Girder made from three 2″ x 10″'s resting on wall with part of the block cut out to receive it.

3. Anchor Bolts.

When you arrive at the top and last course you must set **ANCHOR BOLTS** into the block. These are long bolts which are cemented into the cores every 4 or 5 feet and which are placed so that they protrude in order that the "sills" may be bolted to them when the framing is begun. For this is how the house is attached to the foundation.

A standard 10″ Anchor Bolt.

When the anchor bolts are set all the cores of the top course should be filled with mortar and smoothed level. Take care to set the bolts as straight as possible—it will make it easier to fit the sill over them. Make sure they stick up at least the thickness of the sill you are going to use so that you can get the washer and nut on.

4. Waterproofing.

When all the walls are built, vents installed, provision for girders made as required, anchor bolts set and the top course filled and levelled, the outside wall should be given a good thick coat of "Foundation Coating" which comes in 5 gallon drums from lumberyards. This is not complete protection but it helps and is certainly worthwhile.

In building a house it is seldom possible to do things one at a time in a strict order. Many things will—and should—happen simultaneously, so while this completes the foundation proper there remain a few operations which may also be done at this time, such as the excavation of drainage ditches, the installation of septic tanks and underground services for water, electricity and fuel, and the back-filling of the foundation, etc., all of which, however, will be discussed in Chapter 6.

BIBLIOGRAPHY

Bailey, Kenneth Holmes. MASONRY: A HANDBOOK OF TOOLS, MATERIALS, METHODS, AND DIRECTIONS. New York: D. Van Nostrand Co., 1945

A complete course in all aspects of masonry, from foundations to stucco.

National Forest Products Association. DESIGN OF WOOD FORMWORK FOR CONCRETE STRUCTURES. Wood Construction Data No. 3. Washington: National Forest Products Association, Technical Services Division, 1961

One of an up-to-date series of small handbooks on specific aspects of building. This one is primarily for large structures, but has some useful information on how to make forms and pour concrete.

Ramsey, Charles George, and Sleeper, Harold Reeve. ARCHITECTURAL GRAPHIC STANDARDS. New York: John Wiley & Sons, 6th Edition, Editor Joseph N. Boaz, 1970

This book is an invaluable source for ANY technical detail you may wonder about, from the load that certain size timbers will support to the amount of space necessary for a built-in telephone. In fact, it is considered a standard item in all architects', builders', and designers' offices.

Ulrey, Harry F. CARPENTERS AND BUILDERS LIBRARY. Vols. I–IV. Indianapolis: Howard W. Sams & Co., 1970

These four volumes, formerly known as Audel's Guides, are a set of books covering most aspects of building, with much useful basic information. Particularly useful here is volume III—Layouts, Foundations, Framing.

CHAPTER TWO. *Framing*

This Chapter is divided into four main parts:

    1. Framing Styles, Lumber, Nails & Tools.
    2. Framing the Floor.
    3. Framing the Walls.
    4. Framing the Roof.

1. Framing Styles, Lumber, Nails and Tools.

a. Framing Styles.

Wood is becoming scarcer, the demand is increasing, and consequently the price is rising and the choice diminishing. Time was when only hardwoods were used in the framing of a house—big beams of oak, maple, and chestnut, with mahogany and walnut used for the trim. All these woods are now so expensive that they are used more and more only for furniture and really fine work. Nowadays houses are commonly framed out with softer woods (which our grandfathers used for firewood) such as pine, hemlock, spruce, and fir. Because the available wood has changed, techniques have changed—and sometimes, of course, vice versa. Instead of heavy wooden skeletons such as old barns have, wooden houses now employ a much lighter framework consisting chiefly of pieces of wood no bigger than 2″ x 4″.

There are different methods of constructing such light frameworks, such as **BALLOON FRAME CONSTRUCTION** where the 2″ x 4″'s, known as studs, which comprise the walls, extend in one piece from foundation to roof; and **BRACED FRAME CONSTRUCTION** which is an adaptation of an old English method using heavy corner posts, sills, and plates with small 2″ x 4″ studs in between.

BALLOON FRAME   BRACED FRAME

A third type, explained in this chapter, is called **WESTERN FRAMING.** What makes this different is that the framing for the walls rests on platforms independently framed, i.e. neither the studs, as in Balloon Framing, nor the posts, as in Braced Framing, are continuous from foundation to roof.

A Two Storied Western Framed House.

b. Lumber.

The wood for framing may be bought directly from a sawmill—in which case it is likely to be "green", i.e. unseasoned and undried, but full dimensional and cheaper; or it may be bought from a lumberyard or building supply company, in which case it is almost sure to be "dry", i.e. seasoned and/or kiln-dried, but "dressed" and more expensive.

DRESSED or "milled" means that it has been planed smooth. When lumber comes from the sawmill it has a rough surface, having been cut straight from the tree trunk with one big saw blade—but a piece of wood called "2″ x 4″ " will measure a

A sawmill 2″ x 4″

Square and rough, still showing marks of saw. Heavy because it still contains much moisture

Smooth, rounded, smaller and lighter

A lumberyard 2″ x 4″.

full two inches by four inches. Dressed lumber, which has been planed on all four sides, measures less than the "nominal" size.

Whether you use sawmill "roughcut" or lumberyard "dressed" is up to you. The difference is basically that roughcut is cheaper and dressed lumber more convenient. The most common sizes needed for framing are kept by all sawmills and lumberyards. They are listed below, showing nominal and actual sizes.

NOMINAL SIZE Sawmills	ACTUAL SIZE Lumberyards
2″ x 4″	1½″ x 3½″
2″ x 6″	1½″ x 5½″
2″ x 8″	1½″ x 7⅜″
2″ x 10″	1½″ x 9⅜″
2″ x 12″	1½″ x 11⅜″

Lumber is sold either by the "Linear" Foot or by the "Board" Foot.

LINEAR FEET is simply the length of any given piece. Therefore 30 Linear Feet of 2″ x 4″ is enough 2″ x 4″ to stretch 30 feet. For example, 3 pieces each 10′ long, or 6 pieces each 5′ long.

BOARD FEET is a way of computing the amount of wood in terms of **UNITS** 1 inch thick, 1 foot wide, and 1 foot long.

One Board Foot of Wood.   Half a Board Foot of Wood.

To convert wood of any size other than 1″ x 12″ into Board Feet simply multiply the thickness by the width by the length and divide the total by 144 if all the above dimensions are expressed in inches, or by 12 if one of the dimensions is expressed in feet.

E.g. A piece of wood 2″ thick by 6″ wide and 10′ long.

$$\frac{2″ \times 6″ \times 10′}{12} = \frac{120}{12} = 10 \text{ Board Feet.}$$

$$\text{or } \frac{2″ \times 6″ \times 120″}{144} = \frac{1440}{144} = 10 \text{ Board Feet.}$$

Wood is commonly graded at lumberyards according to how full or clear it is of knots. There are numerous classifications but for all practical purposes only "Number One" and "Number Two" need be considered. Number One is generally free of knots, and Number Two is not!

Framing lumber, such as 2″ x 4″, is generally No. 2—tight knots, sound and usable without waste.

c. Nails

For framing a small house * buy one box each of 10d. Common, 16d. Common, and 20d. **COMMON NAILS.** The "d." stands for penny and indicates the size. It used to be—long ago in England—that 100 10d. nails cost 10 pence, 100 16d. nails cost 16 pence, and so on. The "d." being the old English abbreviation for penny. That time is long ago, but the nomenclature remains, even though nails are now bought by the pound rather than the hundred. "Common" indicates the type—a round, wire nail with a flat head. A box holds 50 lbs.

* up to 1,000 square feet

20d. Common   4″ long

16d. Common   3½″ long

10d. Common   3″ long

Common Nails—Actual Size.

Common nails are made in sizes from 2d. (1″ long) to 60d. (6″ long). They are also made with a galvanized coating—to prevent rust where they will remain exposed. There are many other types of nails, such as Finish, Casing, Box, Roofing etc., which will be discussed as they need to be used.

d. Tools.

Here follows an illustrated list of the tools needed for framing. The circular saw and electric drill assume that there is electricity at the site already. This is not indispensable but VERY labor saving.

Buy and use only the BEST—they work better and last longer. Many times you will be able to find second-hand tools in antique stores which are both cheaper and better made than new tools.

Take care of tools—protect sharp edges and sharpen them often. Keep moving parts oiled. Do not allow tools to get wet and rusty.

There are many specialized types of almost every tool illustrated here, some of which will be discussed when necessary—for framing purposes use types similar to those illustrated.

1. A RETRACTABLE METAL TAPE.

10', 12', 16' or even 20' long.

for measuring.

2. A PENCIL for marking.

3. A WINDABLE CHALK LINE
for marking long straight lines.

4. A CARPENTER'S METAL FRAMING SQUARE

Tongue

Body

This is probably the most complicated tool. Whole books have been written about it. It measures all kinds of angles for rafters, etc, and usually has lots of tables on it. Use it as a big right angle square. The body and the tongue may be 24" and 18", both graduated in inches.

5. A TRY SQUARE

for marking right angles and testing the squareness of wood.

6. A COMBINED TRY & MITER SQUARE

this tool also marks 45° angles.

7. A BEVEL

this can be adjusted to mark ANY angle on a piece of wood.

8. A SPIRIT LEVEL

for measuring the plumbness and the levelness of various surfaces.

9. A PLUMB BOB

for measuring plumbness, for marking a spot immediately below something else.

10. A PORTABLE ELECTRIC CIRCULAR SAW.

for all kinds of sawing.

11. A HAND SAW

13. A 5lb. MAUL *a kind of lightweight, portable sledge-hammer.*

12. A CARPENTER'S CLAW HAMMER

12 oz., 14 oz., 16 oz. or even 20 oz.! the heavier the hammer the quicker it will drive a nail — but the stronger you must be!

14. A CAT'S PAW

for removing nails from tight corners.

15. AN ELECTRIC DRILL

for making holes.

16. A 2' WRECKING BAR

for prying things loose & pulling nails.

18. A ¾" PLASTIC HANDLED WOOD CHISEL

an all-purpose chisel you may hit with a hammer.

17. A JACK PLANE

for smoothing the surface of wood. This is a medium size.

19. A SCREWDRIVER

for screws.

2. Framing the Floor.

The framed floor or "platform" of a Western Framed house consists of:

>   **1.** Girders.
>   **2.** Sills.
>   **3.** Joists.
>   **4.** Sub floor.

1. Girders.

If the side walls of your house are more than 16′ apart, i.e. your house is more than 16′ wide, it will be best to install a girder. A girder is a beam which runs the *length* of the house, and which acts as an additional support for the floor beams—called "joists."

A Girder running the Length of a House.

The girder should be set at least 4″ into the foundation wall. The top of the girder must be "flush" with the top of the sill since the same joists which are going to rest on the sill must also rest on the girder at the same level.

Showing how Girder sits in Foundation Wall.

* See next page for explanation of "flush."

Girders are usually made from 3 pieces of 2″ x 12″ nailed together with 16d. nails. Choose the flattest piece for the center, and if the wood is not perfectly straight make the girder with the "Crown" up. This will counter the weight carried and there will be no sag.

The crown is the highest point on the convex side.

This is very exaggerated; if your board is this bent, discard it and get another.

To find the crown—even a very slight one—sight along the top of the board from one end.

Stagger the joints if the girder is too long to be made out of single pieces.

If the Girder is more than 20′ long it should be supported at its center by some kind of pillar, or pier—like the one shown below.

* FLUSH means "in the same plane".
  A & B are "flush".
  C is "proud", i.e. sticks up.
  D is "recessed" or "rebated", i.e. lower.

Ascertain the length the girder must be—by measuring the distance from one recessed end of the foundation to the other—("x" in the diagram), and make up the girder from 2″ x 12″'s on top of one of the side walls. When it is made just roll it over and into place.

If a center support is necessary it should be built as nearly level with the top of the walls as possible. It is better to build it slightly lower rather than slightly higher since the girder can always be shimmed up if it is not level. In fact a slight crown (of about 1″) is often given to the girder to obviate any settling of the center support.

2. Sills.

The Sill is the timber which runs all around the top of the foundation wall—and is in fact bolted to it—to which the joists, and indirectly the whole superstructure, are nailed. It is thus the link between the foundation and the house on top, and as such it is the most important piece of wood in the house—and the most costly and difficult piece to repair.

For small houses sills may be made from 2″ x 6″. They should be marked and drilled to fit over the anchor bolts set in the top of the foundation in such a way as to be flush with the outside face of the foundation wall.

In order to prevent water filling any unevennesses between the sill and the top of the foundation wall, the sill is sometimes laid in a bed of wet mortar, the nuts on the anchor bolts being tightened down after the mortar has dried. An easier way is to lay the sill on a bed of some other rot resistant material such as fiber glass. This may be bought especially for this purpose in long rolls, 6″ or 8″ wide, or you may cut up your own from regular fiber glass insulation. In any event the sills should be firmly bolted down, level and tight to the top of the foundation and flush with the outside face, and made with pieces as long as possible.

3. Joists.

When the girder and sill are in place, the joists are laid. The joists comprise the frame for the floor, and are nailed to the sill and girder. They are commonly made from 2″ x 10″ (although they may be heavier if they have to span longer distances than 16′) and are placed on edge every 16″.

They are trimmed with "headers" at the ends, and every 8′ or less "bridging" is installed to prevent the joists springing sideways under the load. A better form of bridging is "blocking" made from pieces the same size as the joists. Any openings in the floor (for stairs or a trapdoor) require trimmers—which are simply double joists, and headers. All of these terms are illustrated below.

To lay the joists, start at one END of the building and mark the sills every 16″. Most tape measures are specially marked in 16″ increments to accommodate this often used measurement. If you are proceeding from LEFT to RIGHT, as in the diagram below, the joists will sit just to the right of the marks you have made. Do not worry if the distance between the last two marks is less than 16″.

When you have marked the sill, mark the girder the same way—starting from the same end!

The joists should then be nailed to the sill and the girder in such a way as to leave 1½″ at the sill for the joist header (or box beam as it is sometimes called), and project past the girder at least a couple of inches.

"Toenail" the joist from both sides to the sill at one end and the girder at the other.

TOENAILING with 16d. Common Nails.

It may help to nail two joists to the sill, the distance of one header's length apart first, nail the header to these two joists, and then install the intervening joists, butting them firmly against the header.

1. Nail the 2 joists first.
2. Nail the header to the joists.
3. Nail in the intervening joists.

When all the joists, and headers, are in place on this side of the house, do the same thing on the other side, EXCEPT that the first joist will meet the first joist from the other side head-on and the second joist should be 14½″ away, not 16″, so that it will be next to the second joist from the other side as shown.

Nail the joists where they overlap at the center.

There must be some way into the basement or crawl space, so choose a good spot which is not going to be under a partition wall or a bathtub and plan an opening. By leaving out one joist the opening will be wide enough. Double the joists on either side of the opening—they then become known as "trimmers"—and toenail in double headers as shown. Finally, install the remainder of the intervening joists.

If the joists span 8′ or more (the span is the distance *between* supports) install a row of blocking. Block the ends of the joists over the girder as well.

Cut the blocking ¹/₁₆″ longer than the space between two joists and insert every other one first—as at "A". Then fill in the other ones, keeping the line straight. This method keeps the strain evenly distributed and the joists straight.

Plan of Floor Frame Showing
Blocking.
(Blocking shown as solid lines)

Cross Bridging is often used instead of Solid Bridging (Blocking)—it makes the electrician's job of threading the wires about under the floor much easier, but blocking should be used under partitions and under heavy loads. Cross bridging may be made from 1″ x 3″, although 1″ x 4″ is better. When installing it nail only the top ends—wait until the flooring is laid before nailing the lower ends.

Two 10 d. Nails each end.

CROSS BRIDGING

A Metal Bridging strap which may be bought in place of making up wooden pieces.

4. The Sub Floor.

The Sub Floor is a kind of platform covering the entire length and breadth of the building. It may be made from boards 1″ x 4″, 1″ x 6″, or 1″ x 8″. These boards are laid diagonally. Or, it may be made from a grade of plywood known as plyscord, and should be at least ½″ thick.

Start in one corner and cover the entire area—except, of course, any opening you

Always make joints over joists & NEVER have two joints together.

Two 8d. Nails at each crossing of joist header and blocking. 3 Nails if the board is 8″ or wider.

HEADER

JOISTS

SILL

DIAGONAL SUB FLOOR

may have made. Cut the boards off at a 45° angle (using the combined try and miter square) and always join them on a joist. Use two nails per joist (3, if the board is 8″ or more wide). The ends may be allowed to hang over the edge of the building until the whole area is floored, when they can all be cut off at once. This type of floor is very strong and helps prevent squeaks when the finished floor is later laid.

Plyscord is quicker to lay but may well be more expensive. It comes in 4′ x 8′ sheets and should be laid with the 4′ side resting on a joist. The 4′ sides should never line up; cut one board in half to avoid this, as in the diagram.

PLAN OF PLYWOOD SUBFLOOR

If you are going to use plyscord it is often worthwhile to study the layout of the area to be covered in order to see if with a little ingenuity the sheets may be laid in such a way as to utilize the joists, headers, and blocking as nailing surfaces and leave a minimum of edges unsupported and to make necessary the cutting of as few sheets as possible.

The plywood is nailed every 10″ or so using "Plywood Underlayment Nails", which are made with rings on the shank so they won't pull out so easily.

A RINGED PLYWOOD NAIL

Make every effort to keep the sheets of plywood square with the building and as tight to one another as possible.

3. Framing the Walls.

With the sub floor down, and armed with a floor plan showing the location and dimensions of windows, doors and interior walls (partitions), framing of the walls may begin.

Every house of different design presents its own problems of framing construction, and more particularly, the order in which things should be done. Experience is the best teacher but if the fundamental techniques are understood, a little forethought and common sense will clear away many difficulties.

What follows is a series of illustrations showing how the various details for corners, windows, doors, and partitions etc. are formed.

1. SECTION OF WALL FRAMING.

1. Sole plate nailed through subfloor to joist with 16d. Common Nails, 16″ o.c. (= on center—every 16″).

2. Studs nailed to Sole Plate 16″ o.c. with 10d. Common Nails. Two nails per stud.

3. Top plate nailed to studs 16″ o.c., same nailing.

4. Top plate made of TWO 2″ x 4″'s, the top one nailed to the underneath one *after* the underneath one has been nailed to the studs. Stagger the joints, i.e. do not have the two 2″ x 4″'s comprising the top plate end over the same stud.

5. Cats are 2″ x 4″'s nailed between studs, similar to blocking in the joists. They help stiffen the wall and provide extra nailing surface.

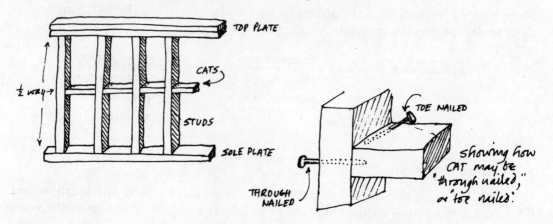

2. CORNERS.

"A" and "B" are methods which may be used if rough-sawn full dimensional 2″ x 4″'s are used.

If dressed lumber is used method C must be used, using a "filler block" every four feet.

A Complete Corner, Showing Filler Block Construction.

N.B. The first stud from a corner should be 15¼″—not 16″—from that corner, to provide nailing space for the sheathing.

3. CORNER BRACING.

Corner bracing is often dispensed with, especially if plywood sheathing is used on the outside, but it is well worth the effort if you live in an area of high winds. In any case in many areas the local building code makes it mandatory. There are two ways of bracing; one is with 2″ x 4″'s forming a triangle with the studs in every corner, and the other is letting a 1″ x 4″ into the outside face of the studs, also at an angle.

Ideally, Corner bracing should extend from the top plate to the sole plate at an angle of 45°. This is rarely possible because of windows and doors, etc. But the closer you can get to this, the stronger it will be.

" 2″ x 4″ BRACING. "

" LET IN BRACING."

1″ x 4″ BRACE

2″ x 4″ STUDS

Nail bottom of brace
into sole plate .

4. WINDOW OPENINGS.

All studding at openings must be double to provide adequate nailing for the trim.

Extra care should be taken to make the openings as square as possible—this will make the installation of the windows much easier.

If the opening is wider than 3' the headers should be 2" x 6"'s; under 3' you may use 2" x 4"'s.

Make the opening at least 3" larger all round than the window to go in it. If in doubt make it bigger since you can always add another stud if it is too big.

5. DOOR OPENINGS.

All of the above applies to door openings too.

The width of the rough opening depends on the method used to trim the door. Remember it has to be as wide as the door, plus the width of both jambs, plus ½" or so for fitting.

If the lumber used is dressed, a ½" piece of plywood inserted between the two pieces of the header will make the header the width of the studs.

6. PARTITIONS.

SOLE PLATE →

INTERIOR WALL →

FILLER BLOCK

← SOLE PLATE

← INTERIOR WALL

A   B

PLAN.

TWO METHODS OF CONNECTING PARTITION TO OUTSIDE WALL.

Partitions are interior walls which divide the building into rooms and passageways. Try to locate partitions which run parallel with the floor joists over joists. If the partitions are to have any load-carrying function—such as supporting part of the roof—the joists should be doubled up.

Leave gap in top stud of outside top plate so that the top stud of the partition top plate may "key" into it.

TOP PLATE →

PARTITION WALL

OUTSIDE WALL

CORNER AS AT "B" ABOVE

Headers over openings in non-bearing partition walls may be 2" x 4"'s since they carry no weight.

When cutting studs, first cut *one* to the correct length (allowing for the sole plate and the top plate), and then use this stud as a pattern from which to cut all the others.

The easiest way to construct framing is in sections, on the floor. This way the sole plate can be nailed to the studs from underneath. Then the whole section is lifted up and nailed to the sub-floor, plumbed with the spirit level and braced.

Check plumb with spirit level before bracing

METHOD OF BRACING A SECTION OF FRAMED WALL.

4. Framing the Roof.

The roof is framed out with **RAFTERS**, which are to the roof as the joists are to the floor, and the studs to the wall. There are many different shapes a roof can be, all of which have different names and all of which require differing techniques of construction.

Although a competent carpenter may be expected to know them all, only a GABLE ROOF is described here. This is among the simplest of styles, and is also probably the commonest, and may be used on almost any type of house.

The main purpose of a roof is to keep out rain and snow, and apart from esthetic considerations this is the most important factor in determining the roof's **PITCH**— the steepness of the roof's slope. In areas of heavy snowfall a steeply pitched roof is desirable as it allows the snow to slide off. And yet a layer of snow is extra insulation and sometimes steepness of pitch is tempered with a heavier construction to withstand and support the extra weight. In other areas roofs are actually built to collect the rain!

A Gable Roof requires only Common Rafters, whereas more complex roofs use such kinds as Hip Rafters, Valley Rafters, Jack Rafters and Octagon Rafters, etc. A Common Rafter rests on the Top Plate of the wall, and against a Ridge Board. Sometimes the Ridge Board is left out. It forms an angle of 90° with the plate.

COMMON RAFTERS ON GABLE ROOFS

Some Definitions.

x = Roof Span

1. THE ROOF SPAN is the shortest distance between opposite Top Plates.

2. THE RAFTER SPAN is the distance between *supported* points of a rafter.

x = Rafter Span

3. THE TOTAL RUN is the *level* distance over which a rafter passes—this is usually half the Roof Span.

x = Total Run.

4. THE TOTAL RISE is the vertical distance from the Top Plate to the Peak (the top of the Roof).

x - Total Rise.

5. THE PITCH of a roof is usually expressed in terms of the RISE in inches per foot unit of RUN. It may also be expressed as a fraction, or in degrees.

For example, a roof which rises 6″ for every foot of run has a 6 in 12 pitch. This is also called ¼ pitch.

RISE in inches	RUN in inches	DEGREES	PITCH
3	12	15°	⅛
6	12	26½°	¼
8	12	33½°	⅓
12	12	45°	½
16	12	53°	⅔
18	12	56½°	¾
24	12	63½°	1

ROOF SLOPES IN RUN & RISE, DEGREES AND PITCH.

This roof is ¼ Pitch; i.e. 12″ in from the plate it is 6″ higher than the plate.
The Total Run is 6′.
The Total Rise is 3′.
The angle at the plate is 26½°.

Before the roof may be framed the following points must be determined:

1. The Pitch.
2. The Size and Spacing of the Rafters.
3. Length of Rafters.
4. The Cuts.

1. The Pitch.

This is a question of balance between the possible snowload, the heaviness or lightness of construction, and the way you want the house to look. For example, if you live in a heavy snowfall area and you want a low pitched roof it will have to be made of heavier construction than it would be if you lived where there was no snow to be borne.

The easiest pitch to build is ½ pitch because then all cuts are 45°. But remember that ½ pitch, or 12″ in 12″, on a wide building necessitates longer rafters than would a smaller pitched roof.

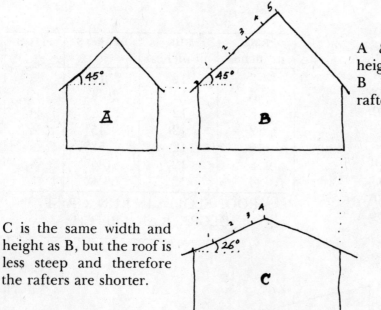

A & B have the same height walls, but because B is much wider, its rafters are much longer.

C is the same width and height as B, but the roof is less steep and therefore the rafters are shorter.

2. The Size and Spacing of the Rafters.

The SIZE of the rafters is a function of the rafter span and the pitch of the roof. This may only be properly computed by reference to tables showing the load bearing capacities and deflection of various woods. For a roof of ½ pitch with a span of around 20′ (rafter span would be 10′), 2″ x 8″ lumber is sufficient for rafters—even when snow must be borne.

Remember though, that the rafter span may be shortened by the addition of a collar beam—a timber from one rafter, horizontally, to the opposite rafter.

The spacing of rafters is usually 16″ on center (one every 16″). The further apart they are, the more they must each carry, and so the bigger they should be.

3. The Length of Rafters.

The length of the rafter may be found using Pythagoras' Theorem—

$$A^2 + B^2 = C^2$$

where A = the Rafter Span, B = the Total Rise, and C = the Rafter.

However, few carpenters carry Square Root Tables around with them, and finding square roots leaves room for error. There is a far simpler method, using the framing square. All that is necessary is to know the total run and the total rise—i.e. the pitch.

Let us assume we are going to build the roof with ½ pitch. The total rise is 10′ and the total run is 10′. Lay the rafter on its side and place the framing square (which, whatever else is marked on it, will have all its edges graduated in inches) so that 12″ coincides with the edge of the wood.

This represents 12″ of rise. Call it point A. Swivel the square around so that the other 12″ mark coincides with a point we shall call B. This represents 12″ of run.

Repeat this, starting from B, and mark C.

If the total run of the rafter had been 2′ you would have now marked off the length—i.e. the distance from A to C. Since the total run is 10′, you must repeat the first step 10 times—once for each 12 inches!

Distance from Point A to Point K is the Length of the Rafter.

SHOWING ALL THE STEPS IN THE LAYING OUT OF THE LENGTH OF THE RAFTER

4. The Cuts.

Rafters must be cut at both ends. Where they meet is called the Top or Plumb Cut. Where they touch the plate is known as the Seat Cut. The part of the rafter which extends past the plate is known (if it exists) as the Tail or Lookout. This may be sawed in different ways depending on whether the Eaves (the overhang of the rafters at the side of the building) are going to be left exposed or whether a cornice is going to be built around them.

If the roof is built with a 12″ in 12″ pitch all the rafter cuts may be marked out with a miter square, since all the angles are 45°.

For roofs of different pitches, and for roofs requiring different rafters with different cuts the use of the Framing Square should be learned.*

Once one rafter has been correctly measured and cut it may be used as a pattern from which to cut all the others.

An easy method of erecting the rafters is by using a RIDGE BOARD. This is a board, usually 1″ x 12″, which runs the entire length of the building and which may be marked off every 16″ corresponding with a similar set of marks on the plates.

When using a Ridge Board subtract half its thickness (⅜″ if it is a nominal 1″ board) from the length of each rafter.

(With the help of friends) erect the end pair of rafters first, nailed at the top to the ridge board. Hold or brace the rafters perfectly plumb—use the level—and

* See Bibliography.

erect a second pair at the other end of the ridge board. Then all the intervening rafters may be slid up over the plate and nailed in place, to both the Ridge Board and the top plate. In order not to push the Ridge Board out of a straight line erect the rafters in pairs rather than all from one side first and then those from the other side.

If the building is too long to use a single board for the ridge, it (the Ridge Board) should be joined between two rafters.

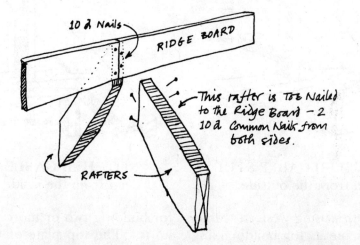

If the rafters are long enough to require Collar Beams (or Ties), they should be the same size as the rafters and nailed to each pair of rafters, level, no further up the rafter than half way.

NAILING DETAILS

When the roof is framed it only remains to frame out the Gables—the area at the end of the roof above the end top plates. The gables are framed out with 2″ x 4″ studs set on 16″ centers like everything else. They are toe nailed into the top plate but may be either beveled under, or notched to, the rafters as shown. Beveling is quicker but notching is stronger.

BEVELED GABLE STUD
Seen from the outside.

NOTCHED GABLE STUD
Seen from the inside.

The procedure, using western framing, for building two or more storied buildings is the same as for building single stories. The top plate of the first floor becomes the sill for the second floor joists and the whole structure is repeated.

For buildings with 3 stories the first floor framing should be heavier, but the principle remains the same.

If there is to be an attic the joists for the attic floor are nailed to the rafters just as are the collar beams, but they rest upon the top plate and are toenailed into it. The second floor joists must span the same distance as the first floor joists. Therefore if a girder was necessary for the first floor, a girder will have to be made for the second floor, seated on studs at the top plate so that the top of the girder is flush with the top of the plate.

Second Floor Girder resting on studs in center of end wall.

Similarly, if the first floor girder required a support in the middle a post will have to be built under the middle of the second floor girder too.

A full discussion of DORMERS (vertical window openings in roofs) is beyond the scope of this volume, for there are almost as many varieties of dormers as there are of roofs. The principles of framing are the same as for other parts of the house.

The Framing of a Shed Roof Dormer in a Gable Roof.

Note that as with openings in the floor or in the walls, dormer openings must have doubled headers and trimmers. For small dormers the rafters may be made from 2″ x 4″ 's. The corner posts should be doubled and both posts and rafters should be 16″ o.c.

BIBLIOGRAPHY

Anderson, L. O. WOOD-FRAME HOUSE CONSTRUCTION. Agricultural Handbook No. 73. Washington: U.S. Department of Agriculture, 1970

A useful government publication. Illustrated orthodox approaches to conventional houses.

Forest Products Laboratory, Forest Research-Forest Service. WOOD HANDBOOK. Washington: U.S. Department of Agriculture, 1940

A really excellent technical book giving "Basic Information on Wood as a Material of Construction with Data for its Use in Design and Specification." 325 pages, last priced at 75¢, of tables, definitions, descriptions and illustrations and very comprehensive bibliographies.

Jones, Mack M. SHOPWORK ON THE FARM. New York: McGraw-Hill Book Company, Inc., 1945

Chapter 8 is an excellent introduction to concrete work; Chapter 3 is one of the best introductions to basic carpentry tools and how to use them. Clearly illustrated.

National Lumber Manufacturers Association. MANUAL FOR HOUSE FRAMING. Wood Construction Data No. 1. Washington: National Forest Products Association, Technical Services Division, 1961

Many illustrations of framing details, from floors to roofs, including staircases.

National Forest Products Association. PLANK-AND-BEAM FRAMING FOR RESIDENTIAL BUILDINGS. Washington: National Forest Products Association, Technical Services Division, 1970

Illustrated details of another system of framing, not so common as standard framing, but with advantages in cost and laborsaving.

Perth, L. THE STEEL SQUARE. New Britain, Connecticut: Stanley Tools, 1949

This little booklet, subtitled "How to Use the Stanley Rafter Square," is the best introduction to the use of the framing square. Lots of definitions and illustrations, 46 pages.

ARCHITECTURAL GRAPHIC STANDARDS (see bibliography at end of chapter 1.)

Sutcliffe, G. Lister, ed. THE MODERN CARPENTER JOINER AND CABINET-MAKER: A COMPLETE GUIDE TO CURRENT PRACTICE. London: The Gresham Publishing Co., 1900

Despite the fact that this large, 8 volume set was published so long ago, it remains the most comprehensive and encyclopedic work on the subject.

CARPENTERS AND BUILDERS LIBRARY (see bibliography at end of chapter 1.)

The Roof Tree

In England, when the "last brick is laid," everybody concerned with the building of the house assembles, from architect to laborer, and a "topping out" party is held—at the owner's expense, with lots of back-slapping and drinking going on.

In Germany, and in fact, in many other countries, similar ceremonies take place when the highest part of the building is complete, and it is from Germany that the American custom of nailing a branch of evergreen to the first pair of rafters to be erected derives. This piece of evergreen is known as the roof tree, and while in olden days it was considered absolutely necessary to propitiate the gods for approaching too closely, it is now considered just good luck. Believe what you will, but do it—it looks nice.

CHAPTER THREE. *Sheathing*

When the framework of the house has been built it is ready for the SHEATH-ING. The sheathing is the outside covering, nailed directly to the studs and to the rafters, to which the final siding and the roofing materials are later applied.

There are operations which might be performed at this point, such as installing doors and windows, and building staircases, but for the sake of clarity these are all described in Chapter 7.

There are several types of sheathing, and indeed, some houses which have no sheathing at all, but the most common, and under most conditions the best, is plywood. Early American wooden houses, and most barns, often simply had the siding nailed directly to the framework and dispensed with sheathing.

A barn with no sheathing, the siding being nailed directly to the framing members.

The next stage was the use of wooden boards, up to one inch thick and from six to ten inches wide, as sheathing; applied either horizontally, or for greater strength, diagonally.

A house sheathed with horizontal boards.

This sheathing should be started from the sill up, and fitted tightly together. Boards should be joined *over* framing members.

Nail boards on with 10d. common nails.

The sheathing on this roof, known as the ROOF BOARDS, is spaced and not tight as on the previous illustration. This may be done if wood shingles are to be used.

Note that the sheathing starts from *both* sides—this is the strongest way. Once again all joints must be made over framing members such as headers or studs.

A house sheathed diagonally.

STRUCTURAL INSULATING BOARD, or SHEATHING BOARD as it is also called, is made in 4' x 8' sheets, like plywood. It is quicker to put up than wood sheathing and is much cheaper than plywood but does not have the strength of either.

There are many grades and thicknesses of plywood. For sheathing, a plywood made with exterior glue is used. If the framing is 16" on center, ⅜" thick plywood may be used for the walls and ½" thick plywood for the roof. However, the use of ½" or ⅝" for the walls and ⅝" or ¾" for the roof is most common because of the extra strength gained and the increased insulation and better nailing surface provided. Plywood sheathing gives great rigidity to the house and eliminates the need for corner bracing.

Plywood should be laid *across* rafters.

On the walls, if it works out better, the sheets may be put on vertically.

Horizontal application is the strongest.

A house sheathed with plywood.

On roofs plywood should be laid crossways to the rafters, as on floor joists, to tie the greatest number of framing members together with one sheet. On the walls, however, it may be installed vertically if this should be more economical and involve less work.

For ½″ to ¾″ thicknesses plywood should be nailed with 8d. common nails, 6″ on center around the edges of each sheet and 12″ on center to the intervening studs or rafters. All joints should be staggered as shown and centered on framing members. Although door and window openings will influence the positioning of the sheets, it is usually best to start from one corner and work along the wall. By nailing the bottom edge of the lowest sheets to the sill, the framework is securely tied to the foundation—since the sill is bolted to the top course of masonry.

If the framing has been erected perfectly plumb and level, then by lining up the edge of the first sheet of plywood with the outside corner it should be possible to place the subsequent sheets tightly against one another, all edges centering on studs. However, discrepancies sometimes arise and the thing to do is to average out the mistake, keeping the joints over the framework, nailing extra 2″ x 4″'s to the studs to provide nailing surface if necessary.

The plywood should come flush to the inside edge of the rough openings (for doors and windows).

PLYWOOD SHEATHING

Sometimes it is more expedient to nail up whole sheets of plywood, disregarding the rough openings, cutting them out later. This often saves time but may result in considerable waste.

To make life easier—but more expensive—it is possible to obtain plywood with jointed edges. This provides greater strength along unsupported edges, but with framing 16″ on center and plywood ½″ thick or more, this is not absolutely necessary.

Tongue & Groove — stronger.   shiplap.

TWO TYPES OF JOINTED EDGES OF PLYWOOD PANELS

The important thing is that the sheathing be as continuous, flat, and tight together as is possible—by using large sections rather than piecing together lots of small bits. Usually, the only difficult part is at the top of the walls, between the ends of the rafters where they extend over the top plate. It may help to place nailers either side of the rafters as shown below, so that the plywood may be nailed more securely.

RAFTERS

NAILERS, nailed to the sides of the rafters with 10d. common nails.

RAFTER TAILS

TOP PLATE

STUDS

PLYWOOD SHEATHING

The nailers may be made from pieces of 2″ x 4″, and should be flush with the top edge of the rafter—as should the top edge of the sheathing.

When sheathing the roof, start at the eaves and work toward the ridge. Lay the bottom sheet so that it projects ⅝″ past the end of the rafter. This will make the CORNICE work easier and better, later on.

PLYWOOD SHEATHING

RAFTER

⅝"

TOP PLATE

STUD

This is the part of the CORNICE (the woodwork which encloses the ends of the rafters) called the FASCIA BOARD which should fit snugly up under the projecting roof sheathing.

At the gable ends (called the RAKE of the roof) the sheathing may extend past the end rafters, but should be supported by pieces of wood called TAILS, toe-nailed to the sides of the end rafters, no more than 4′ apart. Since fascia boards may be nailed to these tails, the sheathing must extend ¾″ over them.

Showing how TAILS, toe nailed to rafters support overhang of sheathing at rake of roof, every 4′.

Ⓐ

SHEATHING

¾" space for fascia board.

RAFTER

10 d. TOE NAIL, 2 each side

RAKE TAIL

A→

RAFTER

TAIL

SHEATHING

Method of framing out corner of rake and eave.

Make the joint at the ridge of the roof as close as is practical, but do not worry if it is not perfectly tight.

The most important thing in sheathing the roof is that the outside edges, at the rakes and the eaves, be as straight as possible, projecting evenly all around. This will make the shingling and the cornice work much easier.

When the whole building has been sheathed, the windows and doors should be installed—this is explained in chapter 7—and then the whole building should be covered with building paper.

BUILDING PAPER (also known as TAR PAPER or FELT) is a black, tar impregnated paper which is water resistant, but not vapor resistant, which helps insulate, windproof and waterproof the building but allows it to "breathe". Rolls of it are made in different thicknesses, or weights; for use under wood siding and asphalt roof shingles the 15 lb. weight is used.

It is applied horizontally, starting at the bottom of the building, successive layers being lapped 4″ or so over the previous layers. Very often, white lines are printed on the paper to facilitate the lining up of long lengths.

Alternatively, a heavy duty stapling machine may be used. This is much quicker, but the staples must be closer together than the nails or the paper will tear off in the wind.

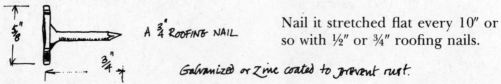

Nail it stretched flat every 10″ or so with ½″ or ¾″ roofing nails.

It is a good idea to try and paper on a mild day. If the weather is too cold the paper becomes brittle and tears easily; if the weather is too hot the paper becomes soft—and tears easily!

If there is to be a long wait before the siding or shingles are applied, and it is at all windy in your area, it will be better to use the roofing nails with ROOFING TINS. These are thin metal discs through which the nails are hammered to help prevent the paper from tearing off the building.

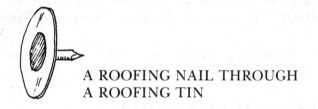

A ROOFING NAIL THROUGH
A ROOFING TIN

The roof is papered * the same way as the walls, taking care to overlap all layers from top to bottom, and the ridge at both sides, so that water runs over the paper and not under.

The reason for installing the doors and windows before papering is that the paper should extend past the edge of the rough opening up to the edge of the door or window frame. This helps reduce drafts.

* If cedar shingles are going on the roof, use ROSIN PAPER instead of tar paper. Rosin paper permits the shingles to breathe and thus last longer.

BIBLIOGRAPHY

American Plywood Association, PLYWOOD SHEATHING FOR FLOORS, WALLS AND ROOFS. Tacoma, Washington: American Plywood Association, 1967
This is only one of the many booklets available from the American Plywood Association covering most aspects of plywood application. Informative and authoritative.
ARCHITECTURAL GRAPHIC STANDARDS (see bibliography at end of chapter 1.)
CARPENTERS AND BUILDERS LIBRARY (see bibliography at end of chapter 1). Volume IV is especially useful concerning the techniques of wooden sheathing.

CHAPTER FOUR.   Siding

The siding is the exterior covering of the walls of a house. It is most usually made of wood, although aluminum siding is becoming increasingly popular because of its long-lasting finish, and more expensive houses sometimes use a veneer of masonry—brick, stone or stucco.

Traditional wood siding may consist of the following types:

1. Plain, square-edged boards nailed horizontally, called CLAPBOARD SIDING.

2. Square-edged boards nailed vertically, narrower strips called BATTENS covering the joints between the wider boards. This form of siding is known as BOARD AND BATTEN.

BOARD AND BATTEN, pine or hemlock, cedar or redwood. The boards may be random widths, up to 12" wide, and the battens are usually 1" x 2" or 1" x 3".

This kind of siding is usually left raw, or stained and treated with creosote—a wood preservative.

3. BEVEL SIDING is most often made from cedar, which weathers extremely well, and so is often left unpainted like clapboarding and board and batten.

BEVEL SIDING

CROSS-SECTION

Common Sizes:

A	:	B
$3\frac{1}{2}$"		$^{15}/_{32}$"
$4\frac{1}{2}$"		$^7/_{16}$"
$5\frac{1}{2}$"		$^9/_{16}$"
$7\frac{1}{4}$"		$^{11}/_{16}$"
$9\frac{1}{4}$"		$^3/_4$"
$11\frac{1}{4}$"		$^3/_4$"

4. CEDAR SHINGLES are also used as siding, particularly in coastal areas because of their resistance to rot. They also come in many grades and sizes.*

(The building paper applied over the sheathing—omitted for the sake of clarity in these illustrations—must not be used with shingles. Instead, ROSIN PAPER must be used—as on shingle roofs.)

5. PLYWOOD PANELLING has become very popular with many builders because of the speed with which large areas may be covered. It is made in many patterns and often requires no treatment such as painting. However, it is expensive to buy although it may save on labor costs.

* See Bibliography.

6. Probably the commonest form of wood siding is DROP SIDING. This consists of horizontal boards, usually painted, shiplapped to fit tightly the one over the other, and made in a variety of sizes and patterns—all basically similar, such as RUSTIC, DROP and NOVELTY SIDING.

CROSS SECTION OF DROP SIDING

SHIPLAP

Most drop siding is made from western pine.

Before any siding can be erected there will be a certain amount of TRIM WORK to be done—how much depending on what kind of siding is used and your own taste. Trim work is the name given to the woodwork around the outside edges of doors and windows, the corners of the house, sometimes the bottom of the siding, and the CORNICE—the woodwork which covers the rafter ends at the eaves and the rakes.

1. The Cornice.

If the rafter ends are to be boxed in, the cornice is the first trim work to be done, since the corner boards and the siding butt up against it, and it is difficult to make a snug fit against something which is not there yet.

Cornices were originally imitative of the stone cornices of European buildings, built to support heavy roofs, and consequently were often very elaborate, consisting of many fancy moldings.

Basically, a cornice consists of the following parts: FASCIA, SOFFIT, FRIEZE, SHINGLE and BED MOLDINGS.

A BOXED (CLOSED IN) CORNICE

The cornice construction details will depend on the length and cut of the rafter tail. A close look at some old elegant wooden buildings will show the extreme variation in cornices.

WIDE CORNICE

CLOSE CORNICE (No overhang)

OPEN CORNICE

The siding extends up between the rafter tails to the underside of the roof sheathing.

If you do build a cornice, the fascia is the first part to make. This must be at least as wide as the rafters, and is usually made from 1″ thick, dressed lumber. If the building is too long for one piece to reach from end to end, the pieces must be butted together over rafter ends. The fascia should fit snugly up under the projecting edge of the roof sheathing, and if the pitch is steep the top edge should be beveled for a close fit—unless the rafter end is cut square.

A BUTT JOINT

Two pieces of wood joined together simply by placing one against the other form a butt joint—hence "butting together".

TWO PIECES OF FASCIA BOARD BUTTED TIGHTLY TOGETHER AT A RAFTER END
(Roof and wall sheathing removed.)

To nail the fascia use two 10d. *galvanized* common nails at each rafter end. This is to prevent the nail from rusting and staining the wood or paint.

What happens to the cornice at the gable ends of the roof depends on how much rake (overhang) there is. The easiest way with an overhanging rake is to continue the cornice up the gable, using the tails which support the rake in the same way as the rafter ends at the eaves.

If the cornice is to be continued up the rake, the corners of the fascia boards may be simply butted or, more nicely, mitered.

PLAN AT A SHOWING BUTTED CORNER

PLAN AT A SHOWING MITERED CORNER

* See previous chapter for framing out corner of rake and eave.

A close look at old buildings will show a wide variety of trim detail at the rake projection for cornices. Many employ some kind of CORNICE RETURN, as shown below.

If the fascia is made so that it projects below the bottom of the rafter, the soffit will be able to be fitted up against it tightly.

Nail the soffit the same way as the fascia, using two 10d. galvanized common nails to every rafter, and butting the joints over rafters. Although the soffit should fit snugly to the fascia, the edge nearest the building is not so critical since it can be covered by the FRIEZE BOARD, usually made from lumber thicker than the siding—in order to form a wider seat for the siding.

Frieze board may
be 5/4" x 4".

NOMINAL	ACTUAL
5/4"	approx. 1³⁄₁₆"
6/4"	" 1³⁄₈"
8/4"	" 1³⁄₄"

FASCIA, SOFFIT, AND FRIEZE DETAILS
AT GABLE

If the frieze is continued up under the rake the corner should be mitered like the
fascia. Nail the frieze to the studs under the sheathing for greatest strength. Once
again, for the nicest work, bevel the top of the frieze board to fit snugly under the
soffit. This is unnecessary, of course, if the soffit is nailed horizontally to a lookout support.

BEVELED FRIEZE

SQUARE FRIEZE UNDER HORIZONTAL
SOFFIT

After the fascia, soffit, and frieze are in place the shingle and bed moldings may
be applied. Shingle molding is nailed to the top of the fascia and covers the joint
between it and the roof sheathing. Functionally, it need be little more than a plain
piece of 1" x 2"; in practice, it is very often a shaped molding, bought from a lum-

beryard or made up specially by hand, using a molding plane—of which there are many types, each producing a different shape—or by a machine, such as a router or a shaper—two power tools designed specifically to cut moldings.

IRON OR BLADE
WOODEN WEDGE, for holding iron firm.

WOODEN MOLDING PLANE

The iron is cut to the same shape as the bottom of the plane; this determines the shape of the molding which is produced.

8d. FINISHING NAIL

RAFTER

1" x 2" SHINGLE MOLDING

FASCIA

"OGEE" STYLE SHINGLE MOLDING

RAFTER

FASCIA

TWO WAYS OF MAKING SHINGLE MOLDING

Bed Molding is the molding which is sometimes added at the meeting of the soffit and the frieze, and like the shingle molding, may be plain or fancy. A common type used by many builders, and in stock at most lumberyards, is CROWN MOLDING.

RAFTER

CROWN MOLDING USED AS SHINGLE MOLDING

FASCIA

SOFFIT

CROWN MOLDING USED AS BED MOLDING

FRIEZE

STUD

QUARTER ROUND MOLDING, often used as bed molding
A = ¼" to 1½"

2½"

8d. FINISHING NAIL – actual size.

These moldings are best nailed in place using 8d. finishing nails every 8" or so.

If the rafter ends are to be enclosed in a cornice, provision must be made now for ventilation. Ventilation is explained in chapter 6 more fully. All that needs to be done now is to drill holes between each pair of rafters—2 holes, 1″ in diameter, are sufficient if the rafters are 16″ on center—and insert a louver in the soffit (between each pair of rafters). This provides free access for air into the roof. The louver (sometimes pieces of screening are used) prevents insects from entering.

VENTILATION

Part of the fascia and roof sheathing removed to show ventilation holes.

2. The Watertable.

Well-constructed buildings have watertables around the base of the siding. A watertable is not absolutely essential but is good practice since it adds to the appearance of the house and helps prevent the bottom of the siding from rotting out by providing a drip edge.

When constructing the watertable, nail the ⁵/₄″ x 4″ piece on first, mitering the corners, and using the level, take great care to make the whole piece perfectly level, because it is this bottom piece which—in the case of drop siding—determines the position of all of the siding above it.

3. The Corner Boards.

The corners of the building should be trimmed out with corner boards, sometimes made from 1″ x 4″, but in better buildings made from ⁵/₄″ x 4″. These boards extend from the watertable (or the bottom of the siding, if there is no watertable) to the frieze board (or underneath of the roof sheathing, if there is no cornice.) There are three methods, shown below.

1. Nail the Corner Boards, butted, the one to the other as shown, OVER the siding.

2. Nail the corner boards to the house, THEN butt the siding up to the corner boards.

3. The most elegant of all three ways is to nail each board so that its outside edge is flush with the corner of the house, and then nail, with 8d. finishing nails, a piece of ¼″ round molding in the very corner.

All three methods may be used for inside corners. Care should be taken, and the spirit level used, to ensure that the corner boards are nailed up *perfectly* plumb.

INSIDE CORNER

4. The Window and Door Trim.

Window and door trim should be made and fitted before the siding is nailed up. This is dealt with fully in chapter 7.

SIDING APPLICATION

Siding, apart from board and batten siding, and plywood siding, is always started from the bottom up.

It should be nailed into the studs or other framing members.

Short lengths should always end over studs.

Two vertical joints should never align.

If it is to be painted, the nails should be punched below the surface with a nail set and the holes filled with a good grade of putty or wood compound. Cheap grades tend to dry and fall out, leaving the nail head to become rusty and spoil the looks.

NAIL SET

HAMMER

NAIL SET IN

SECTION OF
DROP SIDING

Horizontal types of siding should be spaced so that the bottoms of boards run level with the tops of windows and doors. This is easy with clapboarding, bevel siding and shingles since the amount by which each board covers the one below—the lap—may be adjusted to make it all come out right. With drop siding you should measure down from the top of the window and start the bottom board accordingly.

If the sheathing has been put up carefully and level at its bottom edge it will be easy to nail the first siding board on level. In any event it is always a good idea to ensure the siding's horizontalness with the level.

BIBLIOGRAPHY

HOME PAINTING, WALL PAPERING AND DECORATING. New York: Wm. H. Wise & Co., 1951

This book has some excellent illustrations of ladders, scaffolding, and other means of reaching all parts of the outside of buildings. There is also useful information on exterior siding painting and finishing.

ARCHITECTURAL GRAPHIC STANDARDS (see bibliography at end of chapter 1.)

CARPENTERS AND BUILDERS LIBRARY (see bibliography at end of chapter 1.)

CERTI-SPLIT MANUAL OF HANDSPLIT RED CEDAR SHAKES (see bibliography at end of chapter 5.)

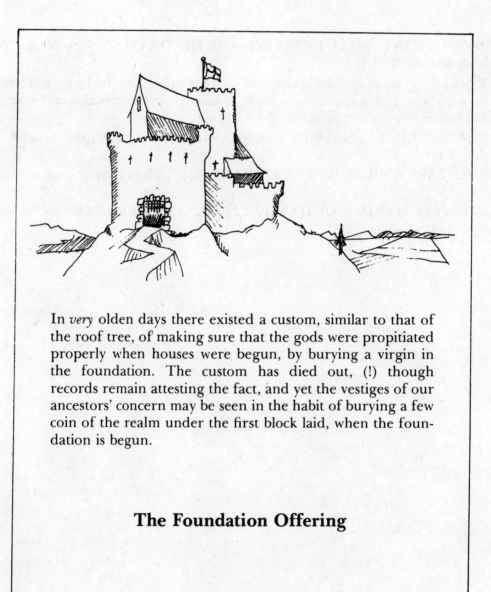

In *very* olden days there existed a custom, similar to that of the roof tree, of making sure that the gods were propitiated properly when houses were begun, by burying a virgin in the foundation. The custom has died out, (!) though records remain attesting the fact, and yet the vestiges of our ancestors' concern may be seen in the habit of burying a few coin of the realm under the first block laid, when the foundation is begun.

The Foundation Offering

CHAPTER FIVE. *Roofing*

Roofs may be surfaced with a variety of materials including metal, slate, clay, wood, tar or straw. The most common roofing material used for small houses is asphalt-felt shingles coated with a layer of mineral granules. This is preferred because of its relative cheapness, quickness of application, and low fire risk. Before describing the application of asphalt shingles, however, mention will be made of some of the other materials. For information concerning the application of these refer to the bibliography.

1. Metal.

Different metals used for roofing include galvanized iron, tin, aluminum, copper, zinc and Monel. While metal roofs are watertight and long-lasting, they are expensive and often annoyingly noisy during rainstorms.

HOUSE WITH TIN ROOF

2. Slate and Tile.

Slate and tile are often used for large, permanent buildings. Slate is more commonly used on stone or brick buildings as it is very heavy but exceedingly long-lasting. Tile, made from burnt clay, and sometimes concrete, is common in the south and west.

MISSION TILED HOUSE

3. Wood.

Wood, riven into shakes and shingles, was one of the earliest roofing materials used in America, and is long-lasting and beautiful but can constitute a fire hazard and also has become very expensive.

A = 16", 18", 24"–27"

SHINGLE:
sawn both sides.

SHAKE:
handsplit one side,
sawn the other.

WOOD SHINGLES:
made from Red
Cedar or Redwood.

4. Straw.

Thatched roofs have been made for hundreds of years and provide a waterproof and well-insulated roof; but they are a BIG fire hazard and tend to harbor insects. Moreover, it is a difficult technique and there are few qualified thatchers left.

THATCHED COTTAGE

5. Tar.

Layers of tar impregnated felt and hot tar provide one of the best coverings for flat and low pitched roofs. This can be a messy business and for regular pitched roofs asphalt shingles are far cheaper and quicker to lay.

6. Asphalt Shingles.

PREPARATION

A number of things must be done before shingles may be applied to a roof. Firstly, the sheathing should be firm and smooth, with no gaps between boards or sheets of plywood, and no nails projecting.

Secondly, for a good job, 15 lb. building paper should be laid, as described in chapter 3. For added quality the paper may be cemented to the edges of the sheathing with asphalt cement—available in 5 gallon cans, and which you will need if there is any flashing to be done.

24" ASPHALT CEMENT

15 lb building paper, lapped 4".

ASPHALT CEMENT

2"

10'

DRIPEDGE

Thirdly, DRIPEDGE is made of galvanized steel or aluminum—which can be obtained painted white. It is made in 10′ lengths and slightly different widths—the wider the better (although 4″ is the recommended width, the most commonly available width is 2″). Its purpose is to support the edges of the shingles, secure the building paper to the roof and most important—as its name implies—to allow the water to drip off the roof rather than run down the side of the cornice and discolor or damage the woodwork.

DRIP EDGE

ROOF SHEATHING

FASCIA

At rake nail dripedge OVER paper.

ROOFING PAPER

At eaves nail dripedge UNDER paper.

To avoid corrosion of the metal through galvanic action, if aluminum dripedge is used, the nails should be aluminum; and if galvanized steel is used then galvanized roofing nails should be applied. In either case nail the dripedge tight to the edge of the roof, using a nail just long enough to go through the paper and the sheathing, about one every 10″. The dripedge is cut easily with tin snips, metal shears or even a hacksaw. When two lengths are joined at the rake, lap the higher piece *over* the lower, so the water runs off and not under.

Fourthly, in preparing the roof for shingling, FLASHING must be installed where necessary. Flashing is usually metal (copper, aluminum, and rarely, tin) in rolls of varying width (10″, 12″, 14″ etc.,) used to waterproof all joints in the roof, such as the intersection of different roof lines, dormer windows, vent pipes, or chimneys.

PLACES WHERE FLASHING IS REQUIRED

Once again, to prevent galvanic action, copper nails should be used with copper flashing and aluminum nails with aluminum flashing. It should be mentioned that copper is many times the price of aluminum, and while it lasts longer than aluminum the cost is usually prohibitive for small houses. In fact while aluminum is sold by the foot length, copper is sold by the pound weight. Flashing should be cut, when it has to go around corners, so that water will run *over* the lower piece and not *under*. It should be set in a bed of asphalt cement (sometimes called roofing tar) with all joints overlapping at least 6″.

When all of the above has been attended to the shingling may start.

Asphalt shingles are made in strips or singles and include the following patterns:

STRIP SHINGLES

SINGLE SHINGLES

Three tab square butt strip shingles are the commonest and easiest to apply. They are sold by the SQUARE. A square of shingles being the amount needed to cover 100 square feet of roof. They are wrapped in packets, 3 to a square. For example, the roof below measures 10′ x 20′. The total square area is therefore 10 x 20 x 2 (because there are 2 sides) which equals 400 sq. ft., or 4 squares, or 12 packets which may be stacked as shown, but never more than 4′ high, or they might squash in the heat.

stack shingles thus

Since wind is any roof covering's worst enemy, the better grades of shingles are provided with a dab of tar underneath each tab which eventually adheres to the shingle below.

There are a wide range of colors available, including black and white. If you plan to have an uninsulated attic remember that white reflects the heat and black tends to absorb it, and would make the attic *very* warm.

APPLICATION

1. Buy a bundle of cedar shimming shingles. These are wooden shingles which are not good enough for the roof (or wall) and are sold in single bundles for all the numerous occasions when things must be shimmed up or out a little. Lay a course (row) of these shingles so that they overhang ½" at the eaves and are ¼" apart (to allow for swelling when they get wet). Nail them with galvanized roofing nails, 2 to a shingle, and take care to keep the edge which projects straight.

2. After a course of shimming shingles has been laid the starter course of asphalt shingles is laid. This consists of a row of shingles laid flush with the edge of the shimming shingles, but upside down. The purpose of the shimming shingles is so that the asphalt shingles may project over the eaves and not sag—as they would eventually do if left unsupported. The purpose of the starter course being laid upside down is to provide a continuous backing for the first course uninterrupted by the slits. It is easiest to start every course from the same end. All shingles should overhang the rake about ½". The first strip of the starter course should be ½ strip, so that the joints of the first course will not lie over the starter course's joints.

3. The next layer is the first course proper. This is laid, right way up, over the starter course, starting with a whole strip. Butt each strip tightly up against the preceding strip so that all the slits will appear equal. Some strips have half a slit at both ends and others have a full slit at one end and a square cut at the other; when all the shingles are laid it should be impossible to tell where the joints are by looking at the slits.

4. The second course of shingles begins with a strip from which ⅓ of the first tab is cut off. This is done so that the joints of subsequent courses never lie directly over one another. The amount of the first course left uncovered should be 5″. This is called "an exposure of 5″ to the weather."

5. The third course completes the cycle, for the fourth course duplicates the first, the fifth the second, and so on. The first strip of the third course has ⅔ of the first tab cut off. (The fourth course starts—like the first—with an entire strip.)

As with tar paper, in hot weather the shingles will tear easily and in cold weather they will become very brittle and crack apart if not handled carefully. The easiest way to cut them is to turn them over and use a framing square and a mat knife as shown:

Make this edge flush and the cut will be square.

You may use any kind of knife but the blade will dull quickly and mat knife blades may be replaced cheaply.

By scoring the shingle deeply it may be folded and broken off cleanly. The reason for turning the shingle over is that if you cut through the mineral granules with which the front of the shingle is coated the knife would wear out much quicker.

To emphasize the main points to remember:

1. The starter course and the first course should be flush with the edge of the shimming shingles which should overhang the roof by about ½″.

2. The shingles should overhang the rake by about ½″.

3. The strips should be butted tightly to one another.

4. The amount of shingle left exposed to the weather depends on the pitch of the roof and the thickness of the shingle. This is usually tabulated on the packet. Thicker shingles are better than thinner ones since they last longer. In general the exposure should be 5″—which is the depth of a slit, which makes it easy to line up the bottoms of each succeeding course with the tops of the slits of the preceding course.

However, every 6 courses or so a measurement should be taken at both rakes and a chalk line snapped between them marking the bottom of the next course, for it is amazing how quickly and by how much the courses can get wavy or out of horizontal and slanted.

When both sides of the roof have been shingled as far as the ridge, the cap course must be made. Cut strips into 3 tabs and nail the tabs sideways, an equal amount on both sides, with the open end away from the prevailing weather.

CUT STRIP

1 TAB   2 TABS   3 TABS

TWO VIEWS
OF THE CAP
COURSE

RIDGE

PREVAILING
WEATHER

RIDGE

A Knurl
Holder

An Undertaker's
Screwdriver

A Carpet Stretcher

Some Tools You Won't Need

GUTTERS

Gutters collect the rain from a roof and lead it to storage—such as a cistern or a rain barrel—to a drain, or simply any place out of the way, thus preventing the area around the house from becoming too wet and soggy.

Wooden gutters are made from rot-resistant woods such as cedar, redwood or fir.

SECTION OF WOODEN GUTTER

Older houses, and large modern buildings often have built-in gutters—built at the eaves *behind* the cornice.

The easiest and cheapest way is to install galvanized gutters; these may be painted, secured to the fascia, or the rafter ends if there is no cornice. Large houses with great expanses of roof require that the gutters and the downspouts be of sufficient capacity to handle the volume of water and that the downspouts be of sufficient frequency to carry it away. Small houses, up to 30' long, are adequately serviced with standard 5" gutters and one downspout.

Gutters may be halfround or "K" pattern:

Downspouts may be round, rectangular, plain or corrugated:

SECTIONS OF DOWNSPOUTS

In cold climates where there is a possibility of standing water freezing in the downspouts the corrugated type is preferable since it will expand without damage. The different parts of a roof drainage system are:

* The strainer is to prevent leaves and other debris clogging up the downspout.
‡‡ Elbows are made in different angles, usually including 45°, 60°, 75° and 90°.

Supports for the gutter are varied and adaptable to different situations. The most usual is a bracket or hanger which is screwed to the fascia and which holds the gutter with a spring clip.

Downspouts are held in place by straps or large hooks nailed to the side of the house.

When hanging the gutters the lengths may be easily cut to length with a hacksaw or a pair of tinsnips. Start from the high end and slope the gutter a minimum of $^1/_{16}''$ for every foot of run. Be careful not to let any lengths slope upwards or pools of water will rest there and rust out the gutter. Use a level to ensure the slope is uniform—the bubble in the vial should be the same amount out of center at all points along the gutter.

The other important point to remember is that the gutter should not project past the roof line.

Otherwise the gutter will impede snow sliding off the roof and an ice dam will result which may force water back up under the shingles and cause the roof to leak.

The steeper the pitch the less clearance is necessary.

12-12 pitch requires ¼" clearance
12-7   "   ½"   "
12-5   "   ¾"   "

When fitting together the various sections of the downspout, fit the upper piece into the lower piece—so that water will run down *inside* the pipe.

BIBLIOGRAPHY

Clark, Donald H. CERTI-SPLIT MANUAL OF HANDSPLIT RED CEDAR SHAKES. Seattle, Washington: Red Cedar Shingle and Handsplit Shake Bureau, 1971

This manual, which may be obtained with much other free material, directly from one of the largest shingle manufacturers, is comprehensive and instructive.

ARCHITECTURAL GRAPHIC STANDARDS (see bibliography at end of chapter 1.)

CARPENTERS AND BUILDERS LIBRARY (see bibliography at end of chapter 1.)

GRAIN LUMBER
Co. INC.

Practically all big lumber companies give these useful aprons away free as advertising.

A CARPENTER'S APRON

Some Useful Equipment

Many lumber yards make saw horses out of their scrap lumber cheaper than you could.

A WOODEN SAW HORSE

A HOUSE FRAMER'S TOOL BOX

Don't try to carry too many tools in these boxes, they get very heavy very quickly & it's hard to find things at the bottom

CHAPTER SIX. *The Works*

This chapter is about things which may be best left to professionals. However, anyone building a house should know at least enough to make the necessary provisions for these various services and in what order they should be done.

The subjects covered are: **ELECTRICAL WIRING, PLUMBING,** and **HEATING.** In addition, **INSULATION, VENTILATION,** and **BACKFILLING** are discussed since these operations must be coordinated with the wiring and plumbing, etc.

ELECTRICAL WIRING

Wiring is in many ways the most complicated and potentially dangerous part of housebuilding, and for these reasons should only be attempted by someone completely qualified.

The best advice that may be given is that proper planning will save time and money, so consult a qualified electrician—in many areas he will be required to be licensed—as soon as possible.

While you will not be able to have electricity in the house until much of it is built, it makes things much easier to have electricity at the site from the beginning. Power may be brought to the site underground or by poles, it being much cheaper to use poles. Pole installation should be arranged with a pole erection company in consultation with yourself and the local utility company. You may have preferences as to the location of the poles based on the view, the erection company will know which is the easiest route in the event of wooded areas or hilly terrain, and the utility company will have its own requirements. Circumstances vary greatly but in general poles are spaced about 150′ apart. They usually belong to you and are your responsibility, but sometimes other arrangements may be made with the utility company or your neighbors.

The last pole before the house should not be more than 125′ away. Its exact location will depend on the site and whether you plan to have underground service to the house or overhead wires.

Your electrician will install a "temporary service" on this last pole and from it you will be able to get electricity while you are building—to run cement mixers, power saws and lights, etc.

From this point the consideration is whether to bring the power to the house over, or underground. If overhead service is decided upon then the siding must be completed so that the "weatherhead" may be fixed to the house.

THE WEATHERHEAD,
FIXED TO THE
OUTSIDE OF THE HOUSE,
THROUGH WHICH THE POWER
LINES ENTER THE HOUSE.

THE WEATHERHEAD, FIXED TO THE OUTSIDE OF THE HOUSE, THROUGH WHICH THE POWER LINES ENTER THE HOUSE.

Every aspect of wiring is carefully governed by the National Electrical Code, and everything must be inspected by the Fire Underwriters Laboratory Inspectors before most utility companies will connect the power. Your electrician will advise you on any provisions which must be made to ensure adherence to the rules—for example, there are minimum heights at which overhead lines may be hung, and stipulations as to where the weatherhead may be affixed—generally to that part of the house closest to the last pole.

Similarly, if you decide to bring the power underground to the house—which is a little more expensive but longer-lasting, safer from weather and other damage,

OVERHEAD SERVICE   UNDERGROUND SERVICE

and better looking,—there are other specific requirements to be met. For example, the cable must be at least 18″ below grade, and if it is to be under a driveway it must be protected in metal conduit.

This is something you should plan together with the excavator and the electrician in order to have all the excavating and covering over again (known as backfilling) done with the least amount of visits by the bulldozer—since this is expensive. The plumber should be consulted at this time too, so that provision may be made for digging trenches to the well or water supply, and installing any wiring needed for a pump.

Ideally, the excavator should dig not only the foundation, but all service trenches and drainage systems at the same time. When the foundations are built, the power lines, drains and septic tanks, etc., should be installed so that everything may be backfilled at the same time.

The first place the power goes in the house is to the distribution box, which is where all the various circuits begin, and where the fuses or circuit breakers,* including the main switch, are to be found. This is also called the loadcenter or panel box.

A CIRCUIT BREAKER
LOAD CENTER

x increases with the number of circuits.

Once again, there are specific requirements regulating its size, type and location. Your electrician will advise you, but you should plan all your needs in advance to determine what size box you will use. For example, a small house might be adequately served by a 100 amp service with 24 circuits, while a larger house, or a house with more electrical appliances, may need a 200 amp service with 42 circuits.

On the next page is a list containing many of the appliances you may want, now or in the future, and a careful consideration of these will enable your electrician to decide on the best size service for you.

* Almost all new installations now employ circuit breakers—which are switches that trip off when overloaded and need only to be switched back on again, instead of the old type of fuses which need to be either mended or replaced entirely.

Air conditioner	Juice extractor
Attic fan	Mixer
Clothes dryer	Oil burner
Dishwasher	Percolator
Disposer	Radio
Egg cooker	Range
Electric fan	Refrigerator
Freezer	Sunlamp
Furnace blower	Television
Grill	Toaster
Hair dryer	Vacuum cleaner
Heating pad	Waffle iron
Hot plate	Washing machine
Infra-red lamp	Water heater
Iron	Wringer

Some Possible Household Appliances

Most panel boxes are made so that they will fit between studs 16″ on center and be flush with the interior wall. It is a good idea to locate the panel box in a closet or in the basement with a removable panel or open space below it so that extra wiring may be added without destroying the wall every time.

When the panel box has been installed the electrician will run the wires around the house—through the walls and ceilings and under the floors—according to the wiring plan. He will install the outlet boxes for receptacles, lights, and switches at convenient places—normally about 14″ high for convenience outlets and 4′ high for switches. Outlets in the kitchen and bathroom and other special areas such as work rooms will vary and must be planned in accordance with your needs and the Code.

OUTLET BOX NAILED
TO WALL STUD

A few points to watch for are:

1. The wire should run through the *center* of the studs, and you must be careful not to nail through the wire later when applying inside, or outside, wall coverings.

2. Wire running around bathtubs should be *below* the top of the tub to eliminate any chance of making contact with the wiring when subsequently putting long screws in the wall for soap dishes or towel racks, etc.

3. Wires should not run too close to the plumbing in order to avoid damage from the plumber's blow torch when he is working.

4. The electrician must know how you plan to finish the walls so that he may set the boxes to project the right amount through the finish wall.

5. Recessed bathroom cabinets, medicine boxes, and vanities all require advance planning in order that the walls may be adequately framed to receive them—some are too wide to fit between studs 16″ on center.

After all this has been done—known as the roughing out—the electrician will contact the Underwriters Laboratory Inspector who will inspect everything, and if satisfactory will issue a certificate and notify the utility company who will then connect the power to the house. At this point you will have at least one outlet with power in the house.

Then the walls may be insulated and covered, and the electrician will wire all the different receptacles in the outlet boxes.

A DUPLEX
RECEPTACLE   A SWITCH

When everything is complete another inspection must be made before the final certificate is issued. This certificate from the Underwriters Laboratory is required by banks for loans and mortgages, and insurance companies, so you must obtain it.

As well as the wiring described above there are other wiring jobs which should be planned at the roughing out stage. These include:

> Thermostat wiring for heaters
> Telephones may be pre-wired at this stage
> Antenna wiring & cable vision wiring
> Hi-fi speaker systems
> Intercoms
> Doorbells
> Central vacuuming systems
> Air conditioners
> Exhaust fans
> Fans for heatilater fireplaces

PLUMBING

While plumbing is not as inherently dangerous as electrical work, it can often cause greater inconvenience if improperly installed or, in cold areas, insufficiently insulated. Moreover, many communities forbid certain jobs to be done by anyone except a licensed plumber. While the purpose of this section is not to dissuade you from attempting your own plumbing, it does not explain the techniques or intricacies involved, but simply provides you with sufficient awareness of the various jobs to be able to plan your plumbing intelligently with the help of a professional plumber.

A PLUMBER'S PIPE WRENCH

The plumbing of a house consists of three main parts: getting the water to the house—**SUPPLY,** draining the water and waste from the house—**DRAINAGE,** and all the work in between—**FIXTURES.**

1. Supply.

The source of supply may be the public mains in urban areas, or private wells or springs in rural areas. The first will certainly have local codes and regulations attached, which if adhered to will ensure a proper and adequate supply. The second may not be governed by any ordinances at all, and it will be advisable to seek local professional advice.

Wells are the most common form of water supply in the country, although sometimes springs and running water may be used to advantage. Since most modern wells are drilled with specialized equipment that can penetrate even rock easily, the location of the well is often simply a matter of convenience to the well driller, but in areas where the sub strata is irregular it has often proved useful to employ a water dowser to determine where the well should be dug. A difference of a few feet may mean a substantial saving in drilling costs.

In general the well should be as close to the house as possible, and as far away from the disposal system as possible—and preferably uphill from it. Also, take into consideration the possibility of future disposal systems which future neighbors might install, and also the fact that presently uncontaminated sources of water may not always remain so—therefore locate your well at least 50' away from any surface body of water.

Once the well is dug you should have it tested for purity, color, and taste. Very often local health codes mandate this, in any case it is rarely worth taking a chance. Find out whether the water is hard or soft. If it is hard you may want to install a water softener, for hard water is difficult to lather and can cause scaling and eventual clogging of pipes. Soft water, on the other hand, often tastes bad.

The amount of water needed depends on the size of the house (measured in terms of the number of bedrooms) and the size of your family. Average consumption may be anything from 50 to 100 gallons per day per person, and may be much more if washing machines and dishwashers etc. are used. The well driller will tell you when the well will produce sufficient for your needs.

AN ADJUSTABLE WRENCH

In most cases a pump and pressure tank are required. Modern submersible pumps installed at the bottom of the well are electrically operated and so their installation must be coordinated with the electrician. Similarly, pressure tanks, which act as storage tanks and control the pump motor, are also electrically wired. The most important point here is to install a large enough tank so that the pump does not start operating every time a faucet is turned on.

A 42 GALLON PRESSURE TANK

The water may be piped to the house in metal or plastic pipe. Plastic is much cheaper but is sometimes prohibited by code. In either case the pipe should be buried carefully so that it will not be crushed by rocks and damaged.

Whatever else you do, make sure that this supply line is *ADEQUATELY INSU-LATED* if there is any danger of freezing weather in your area. This may be achieved by burying the line below the frost line, lagging (wrapping) it with insulating material or the judicious use of heat tape—electrically heated wire wrapped around the pipe. It doesn't matter how good the rest of your plumbing is if the supply line freezes in mid winter. Frozen pipes are expensive to thaw and can cause a lot of damage if they burst.

2. Drainage.

Once again, because drainage systems may vitally influence the health of the entire community, there are often stringent regulations governing such systems.

The best individual sewage system is the septic tank and drainage field. This consists of a house drain, a septic tank, an outlet sewer, a distribution box, and a disposal field.

HOUSE DRAIN

OUTLET SEWER

5" DIAMETER CAST IRON PIPE

SEPTIC TANK (CONCRETE OR METAL)

DISTRIBUTION BOX

A TYPICAL SEWAGE SYSTEM

DISPOSAL FIELD

PERFORATED FIBRE DUCTS

The location will be partly determined by the lay of the land—since the drainage should be preferably downhill and away from the water supply. But remember that you may need access to the septic tank in the event it needs servicing.

The SOIL PIPE is the main drain from the house to the septic tank. This is

PITCH TOO STEEP
Pipe tends to clog

NORMAL PITCH makes the pipe self-scouring by reducing the run off speed of the liquid waste.

Recommended pitch = 1" per 4'.

usually made from 5″ cast iron pipe and must be pitched at the right slope. If it is too steep waste will accumulate in the pipe.

The SEPTIC TANK is either tar-coated steel or concrete. Concrete costs more but lasts longer. The raw sewage enters the septic tank and bacterial action breaks the solids down into gases and liquids which drain off to the disposal field. The size of the tank is important, for a tank which is too small will soon become overloaded with sludge and may back up into the house.

NUMBER OF BEDROOMS	NUMBER OF PERSONS SERVED	CAPACITY OF SEPTIC TANK IN GALLONS
1 or 2	no more than 4	350
3	no more than 6	550
4	no more than 8	600
5	no more than 10	750
6	no more than 12	1,000

AVERAGE SEPTIC TANK CAPACITIES
(IMPORTANT: check local codes, they may require larger tanks)

The OUTLET SEWER is the pipe which connects the septic tank to the distribution box.

The DISTRIBUTION BOX is a small tank which distributes the liquids from the septic tank to the disposal lines of the disposal field.

The DISPOSAL FIELD consists of two or more lines of drain tile or perforated fibre pipe through which the sewage liquid seeps into the surrounding ground where it is decomposed by bacteria, completing the disposal process.

A SECTION OF CLAY DRAINAGE TILE

A SECTION OF A LENGTH OF PERFORATED FIBRE PIPE

The number and length of disposal lines depends on the size and occupancy of the house and the type of ground. For example, a large house on a clay site will

TYPE OF SOIL	LINEAL FEET PER BEDROOM
Gravel	40 feet
Sand	60 feet
Loam	90 feet
Clay	160 feet

LENGTH OF DISPOSAL LINE REQUIRED
ACCORDING TO TYPE OF SOIL

require much more disposal line than a small house in more porous ground such as sand.

The slope and size of the trenches to be dug for the disposal lines is also very important, and depends on the type of soil and the contour of the land. This is something which must be planned with the excavator who will dig all the holes and trenches; ideally, at the same time as the foundation is excavated.

The recommended slope is about 3" per 100'. Individual lines should not be longer than 100'. At least two should be laid, even though less than 100' is necessary—in case one line becomes temporarily waterlogged. The line should be about 18" below ground, and if in non-porous soil it should be laid in a gravel filled trench, the whole being covered with a layer of straw or building paper to prevent clogging.

CROSS SECTION OF DISPOSAL TRENCH

Many houses use a separate tank for washing machines, as too much water in the solid waste tank might impair the bacteriological breakdown; not to mention the inhibiting factor of non-biodegradable detergents.

3. Fixtures.

Fixtures include sinks, tubs, showers, water closets * and even outside faucets. Planning with the plumber is the most important aspect of this work. The location of the water heater, the route the hot and cold water lines will take, adequate stopcocks and drain valves are among the things to be considered.

STOPCOCK (CONTROL VALVE, OR GATE VALVE)—when closed the flow of water is stopped completely.

STOP & DRAIN VALVE This valve can stop the flow as the stopcock does, but it can also allow the water from side "B" to drain from the drain valve.

It helps to keep as much of the plumbing as possible concentrated in one area of

* Usually called toilets by the layman; the plumber calls the whole room the toilet.

the house—hot water will cool off if it has to stand, or travel long distances between supply and outlet; the economy in piping achieved through careful planning may also be considerable. Every fixture should be able to be turned off independently, and the whole system should be capable of being drained easily.

Copper is still the best material to use, although better, and adequate, grades of plastic are being developed all the time, and plastic is much cheaper than copper.

One very important aspect to check on is that the whole system is adequately vented. This is necessary to prevent sewage gases from entering the house and to permit quick draining. Proper venting is all too often neglected, and is rather more complicated than merely installing one vent stack (pipe). Make sure that a competent plumber takes care of this. If the vent stack, or stacks pass through the roof, you will have to make sure they are flashed correctly, for this is a major source of roof leaks.

TWO METHODS OF FLASHING THE VENT STACK AT THE ROOF

The plumbing, like the wiring, should be roughed-out when the house has been framed so that all pipes and lines may be chased (built in) in the walls. This is another reason for planning ahead of time in consultation with the plumber.

Separate from the plumbing but to do with water, is the provision for drainage of the ground around the house. When the foundations are complete, drainage tile or perforated fiber pipes should be laid in a bed of gravel all around the base of the footings in such a way as to drain off to the lowest point. The gravel should be covered with a layer of building paper (to prevent clogging) and then the ground may be carefully back-filled to slope away from the house.

HEATING

Houses may be heated by electricity, hot water, hot air, kerosene, coal or fire-wood.

1. Coal and Wood.

The use of coal or wood requires either a fireplace or a stove. Wood (or coal) burning stoves can be very effective and economical, and, in fact, kept America warm for years. But they tend to be dirty and time consuming. It's all right if you only plan to use the house for weekend hunting trips, and like to chop wood, but for permanent living the inconvenience of getting up every six hours throughout the winter to stoke the stove cannot compare with the ease of merely adjusting a thermostat.

THE POT BELLY
WOOD STOVE

However, as an auxiliary system in case of a power failure, or just for the comfort and cheeriness of sitting around a glowing stove or an open fireplace, it is to be highly recommended. Iron stoves are relatively simply installed. Efficient fireplaces that give off heat and do not smoke the house out every time the wind changes direction require a lot of knowledge and skill to build. If you plan to have a fireplace employ an experienced mason, or study fireplace construction thoroughly first. You will need to understand such things as flue sizes, fire boxes, the proper founding of hearths, the corbeling of smoke chambers and correct chimney dimensions.

2. Kerosene.

The use of kerosene space heaters is on the wane since they too can be dirty and are considered a fire hazard. Many insurance companies will not write policies for houses heated this way. However, if kept very clean and provided with an adequate chimney they are certainly efficient heat givers. The important thing about the chimney—as with all chimneys—is that it be at least 2′ higher than the highest part of the roof in order to draw properly and not smoke you out.

3. Gas.

Gas heat is not very efficient and is very expensive. Avoid it.

4. Electricity.

Electric baseboard heat is the cheapest automatic system to install since there is no ductwork, expensive furnace equipment or chimney involved. Every room may

AN ELECTRIC BASEBOARD UNIT
INSTALLED UNDER A WINDOW

be separately controlled and it is a clean and silent form of heat BUT—the house must be insulated very well or otherwise the electricity bill will be enormous.

The baseboard units are normally installed under windows and are of various sizes. If you intend to use this kind of heat your electrician can advise you on the size and quantity of units necessary, and you should plan the location of shelves and closets accordingly, remembering that you will need a certain amount of clear wall space in every room.

5. Hot Water.

Hot water heat is often considered the most comfortable kind of heat. It requires a heating plant of some kind to heat the water—usually an oil-fired furnace—and a series of baseboard units similar to the electric units, although the hot water units are all connected whereas the electric units are separate. It is not a dry heat and so is very comfortable although the noise of the water running through the pipes may be annoying.

Radiators are another form of hot water heat—their main disadvantage being their size and the space they take up. Also you must take precautions against ever allowing the house to freeze, or the radiators will burst if not drained, which can cause a lot of damage.

A TYPICAL HOT WATER RADIATOR

6. Hot Air.

Hot air heat is achieved by using a furnace to heat air which is forced through ducts and out of registers or grills in the floors or walls. This is the least conspicuous form of heat and if used with fiberglass duct work it can be very quiet, unlike the transatlantic liner noises often associated with metal ductwork. By using fiberglass, a humidifier and central air-conditioning may also be built into the system providing a very efficient and sophisticated form of "internal atmospheric control".

Both hot water and hot air systems should be planned and installed by qualified heating engineers—who are often also plumbers. The only carpentry involved is the installation of grills through which the heat passes—illustrated on the next page—and occasional provision for the ductwork.

FRONT VIEW OF HEAT
REGISTER IN FLOOR

SIDE   VIEW   SHOWING
HOW   GRILL   FITS   INTO
THE BOOT OF THE DUCT

Any heating system using a furnace will require a fuel tank to hold the oil which
fires the furnace. It is always economical to have the largest one possible since
fuel rates diminish the more you buy at one time. It may be possible to install the
fuel tank in the basement or you may prefer to keep it outside the house. Tanks
are made to hold 275 gallons, 500 gallons or 1,000 gallons and may be stood on
the ground or buried conveniently underground with just the filling pipe sticking
up. If burying the tank seems like the best idea (it is after all not a pretty object)
plan this well in advance so that the necessary excavation may be performed with
all the other excavating work.

OIL TANK KEPT IN BASEMENT OR CRAWL SPACE

1,000 GALLON OIL TANK BURIED FAR FROM HOUSE BUT
WITHIN EASY REACH OF THE LARGE OIL DELIVERY TRUCKS

INSULATION

No matter what form of heat is used, the house will be much warmer if it is well insulated. Indeed, insulation works both ways and will not only keep the house warmer in winter, it will keep it cooler in summer. Thus it will save money on your heating bills *and* your electricity bills if you use air conditioning.

Thermal insulation is anything which prevents or reduces heat transference from one area to another, such as from the inside of a house to the outside. Every barrier between the inside and the outside has some insulating value, even the sheathing and the siding, but some materials have a much higher resistance than others. The insulating value of a material is referred to as its R factor—the higher the R factor, the better the insulation. Some idea of the difference between R factors may be gained by observing houses with approved insulating material in winter and houses without.

House A has no insulation and the heat from the building has escaped through the roof, melting the snow—but leaving snow at the eaves and rake overhangs, which are not exposed on the underneath to the building's heat. House B has lost no heat through the roof and the snow has remained, unmelted—and incidentally forming an extra layer of insulation.

Structural insulating board which may be used instead of sheathing is probably the cheapest form of insulation, although it has a relatively low R factor.

A comparatively new form of insulation is the use of different plastics—styrenes and urethanes, which are made in such a way as to trap hundreds of small air spaces within them—a dead air space being good insulation. Polystyrene, with the use of proper equipment, may be sprayed onto, or into, a building, and has the advantage of a high R factor in relation to its thickness. Other materials require a much greater thickness to attain the same R factor. It can also be obtained under various trade names in 4' x 8' and 2' x 8' sheets in thicknesses of ½" to 2" with R factors of 4 to 8 respectively.

Another form of insulation is the loose, granular kind, sold in sacks or bags, which is simply poured into the walls between studs. This is most often blown through holes drilled in the sides of existing buildings which were built without insulation. It may also be used in attic floors by pouring it between the attic joists.

The commonest kind of insulation is strips of fiberglass. This is made in short lengths, called batts, or rolls, of varying thicknesses, widths and lengths. Both batts and rolls may also be obtained with a paper or aluminum foil backing. The backing increases the R factor somewhat, but its main purpose is to act as a vapor barrier, necessary to prevent condensation forming between the ceiling and the roof.

FIBERGLASS INSULATION

A PAPER BACKED PIECE OF
FIBERGLASS INSULATION

Since heat rises, the heat loss in a house is greatest through the roof, and least through the floors. Therefore there are different thicknesses of insulation for installation in the roof, walls and floors, each with a different R factor.

	THICKNESS	R FACTOR
Ceiling	6″–6½″	R19–R22
Walls	3″–3½″	R9 –R11
Floors	2″–2¼″	R6 –R7

TYPICAL THICKNESSES OF FIBERGLASS INSULATION,
THE RESPECTIVE R FACTOR, AND
WHERE IT SHOULD BE USED

Fiberglass rolls are made in 50′ and 100′ rolls, batts are commonly 4′ long. Both batts and rolls are made in various widths: 15″, 19″, and 23″, designed to fit between framing members 16″ and 24″ on center.

Backed insulation should be applied with the backing toward the interior of the house; it is commonly either stapled flush with the framing members, or recessed ¾″ to 1″, thus providing the extra insulation of a dead air space when the finish wall (or ceiling) is applied.

TWO METHODS OF INSTALLING INSULATION

Another way of insulating which sometimes saves time and money is to use unbacked batts, and sheets of plastic. The batts are simply wedged into place between the studs or rafters, needing no staples to hold them, and then plastic is tacked over the whole to form the vapor barrier.

Floors may be insulated with fiberglass as shown below:

An easier method is to use an insulating fiber board, made in sheets like plywood, which may be laid directly over the joists, or between the subfloor and the finish floor. In either event the fiber board will require little nailing since the flooring will hold it adequately in place.

FIBER BOARD INSULATION LAID DIRECTLY ON JOISTS
—in which case the edges of the sheets should lie over the joists

FIBERBOARD INSULATION LAID BETWEEN THE SUBFLOOR AND THE FINISH FLOOR

If you are using rolls of insulation it is easiest to cut it to length *before* installing it. Cut it with a mat knife and cut from the backing side. Insulate *after* the plumbing and wiring have been roughed in.

Whether you insulate the basement and attic or not is unimportant—but the living space must be completely insulated.

VENTILATION

If a house is warm inside and cold outside, and there is sufficient humidity within the house, this humidity will condense on contact with the cold surface of the house. This is usually most noticeable at the roof. Similarly, cold and damp air rising from the ground underneath the house will condense on contact with the floor joists. All this moisture would eventually cause the wood to rot, so steps should be taken to prevent condensation from occurring. This is achieved by ventilating adequately all parts of the building where condensation is likely to occur.

PROPER VENTILATION AL-LOWING AIR CIRCULATION THROUGH HOUSE

In the basement, or crawl space, ventilation is achieved by providing vents in the foundation walls as described in chapter 1.

In the roof—the other main danger area—even when a vapor barrier has been used, condensation may still occur, so all parts of the roof behind the insulation should be thoroughly ventilated. Here, all that needs to be done is to provide for an air flow between the rafters, under the sheathing and behind the insulation.

At the eaves this is done by drilling holes and inserting screened louvers—as explained in chapter 4. At the ridge the easiest way is to pull the insulation down into the attic floor and vent the remaining area (above the attic floor) by means of louvered vents in the gables.

The vents for the gable may be made of aluminum. Lumberyards usually carry a good selection of different shapes and sizes. They are mostly flanged to fit simply into a hole cut in the siding the same size.

It is also possible to use small wooden louvered shutters or louvered doors and make a window frame, as described in the next chapter, and insert this.

If you make the louver yourself from a shutter, do not forget to tack some wire screening to the back to keep out the wasps and other insects.—The aluminum factory-made louvers have the screening already in.

If you plan to use all the roof space inside, right up to the ridge, and do not want even the smallest attic floor, then somehow you must allow the air rising up between each rafter to circulate, for venting only at the eaves allows air to enter but does not provide for a free flow—and condensation will result. There are factory built aluminum ridge vents which may be installed when the roof is being sheathed, or you may build your own, as shown below. But the best method for a house with fiberglass insulation between the rafters and finished ceilings is to allow for an attic space at the ridge.

BACKFILLING

Backfilling is the filling in or covering over of all the excavation which may be necessary. There are so many different things to be dug or backfilled that it is a good idea to list everything in one place.

You will need the excavator for the following holes and ditches—all of which may be dug at one time (and all backfilled at one time) if you plan everything far enough ahead:

1. The main excavation for the foundation. (Below the frostline.)

2. The trench to the septic tank. (18″)

3. The hole for the septic tank. (Deep enough so the septic tank, whatever size it is, may be covered by a foot or so of earth.)

4. The trenches for the disposal lines. (18″)

5. The trench for the electric power line—if you decide to have underground wires. (18″—but remember they must be in metal conduit if they pass under a driveway.)

6. The telephone wires may be installed in the same trench as the power line.

7. The trench from the water supply to the house, which will contain not only the water line but the electrical wiring for the pump. (Below the frost line—this is very important if you don't want to dig it up every winter.)

8. A hole for any fuel tank you may want to bury—oil or gas. (Below ground but with the filler pipe above ground!)

9. A trench for the fuel line from the tank to the house. (18″)

10. A run off ditch for any foundation drainage.

11. Trenches for any culverts * that may be necessary under the driveway.

---

* A culvert is a pipe large enough to carry a stream under a driveway. If you need culverts remember to buy them on the basis of the size of the stream when it has most water flowing—many streams big enough to wash away a driveway dry up completely sometimes.

It may well help, before you start to build, to draw a sketch of the building site and show the proposed location of everything on it as in the sketch below. Not only may the local building code require one, but it will help you organize the work better, and eliminate the possibility of forgetting something.

Map of Building Site, showing Proposed Location of all Excavations & Utilities

BIBLIOGRAPHY

NAHB Research Foundation, INSULATION MANUAL: HOMES, APART-MENTS. Rockville, Maryland: National Association of Home Builders, 1971
Probably the best and most definitive manual on insulation yet published. All the facts and figures.

National Lumber Manufacturers Association, INSULATION OF WOOD-FRAME STRUCTURES. Washington: National Forest Products Association, 1964
Contains useful maps and illustrations and a full bibliography of books on insulation.

Nowack, John F. ELECTRICAL WORK, A HANDBOOK OF TOOLS, MATE-RIALS, METHODS, AND DIRECTIONS. New York: D. Van Nostrand Co., 1945
An easy to read introduction to electricity in the home.

NATIONAL ELECTRICAL CODE, Chicago: National Board of Fire Under-writers.
The complete legal specifications for all types of electrical work.

Schaefer, Carl T., and Smith, Robert E. HOME MECHANICS. Milwaukee: The Bruce Publishing Co., 1961
A useful book for understanding the basic principles and maintainance of "the works".

Wolf, Ralph T. THE WISE HANDBOOK OF HOME PLUMBING. New York: Wm. H. Wise & Co., 1953
A well-illustrated basic guide to all aspects of home plumbing.

As well as customs and ceremonies associated with housebuilding, there are also many time-honored tricks played by tradesmen to ensure payment. One such trick was the mason's habit of building a pane of glass across the chimney, high up in the flue. The glass being clear, no obstruction could be seen, but the fire would not draw until the mason was paid—when he would then simply drop a brick down the chimney!

Paying the Mason

CHAPTER SEVEN. *Interior Finish*

The interior finish of the house consists of installing the windows and doors, covering the ceilings and walls, and laying the floors.

1. Windows.

Windows may be divided into three classes: 1. Fixed Windows—which do not open; 2. Casement Windows—which open by having one side hinged to any side of the frame; they may open inwards or outwards, and be hinged from the top, sides or bottom; and 3. Sash Windows—which open by sliding up or down and are held open (or closed) by friction, pins or counterweights. (There are also sideways sliders.)

Theoretically the fixed window is not really a window since the origin of the word implies a hole through which not only light but air may pass. Saxon buildings had no chimneys—merely a hole in the wall or roof—the "wind eye"—through which the smoke escaped and fresh air came in.

All kinds of windows may be bought as ready made units from a number of manufacturers, in many different shapes, styles and sizes. All that needs to be done is to order the right size, place it in the rough opening, and when the inside walls are covered and the outside walls are sheathed, secure the window in place by nailing the trim (or casing) to the window frame and the inside and outside walls.

Such units often have many advantages: they come complete, with storm sash for extra insulation in cold climates, and screens for the insect-laden summer months; all the hardware is affixed—hinges, handles, locks, etc.; and they are quick and easy to install.

The alternative is to buy sash—the part of the window that actually holds the glass—and make your own frames. This has the advantage of being much cheaper, and gives you the opportunity to tailor each window to your particular needs without sacrificing any quality control.

A third possibility is to obtain complete or partial second-hand units from breakers' yards, old houses being torn down, auctions or second-hand building supply yards. There are many such places, and the materials thus obtained are very often superior in quality, if sometimes less sophisticated, and far cheaper than can be bought new.

If you decide, for reasons of economy or quality, to make your own window frames, the simplest form to make is an outward opening casement window. This consists of the following parts:

PARTS OF A WINDOW

Again, the sash is the part which holds the glass—if there are lots of panes of glass in the sash, it is described as a 6 light, 9 light or 12 light window according to however many panes there are. The frame is the part that holds the sash, and the trim (or casing) is the part that holds the frame in the wall.

PARTS OF A WINDOW FRAME

MAKING THE FRAME & TRIM FOR
A CASEMENT WINDOW:

1. Measure the width of the rough opening, i.e. "x" in the illustration below.

2. Cut a piece of $^5/_4''$ thick lumber as shown below: (This is the head.)

The length should be the measurement "x" from the rough opening less $^1/_8''$ so that it will fit easily.

The width, "y", equals the width of the studs, plus the thickness of the exterior sheathing and the interior finish wall plus another $^1/_8''$ for irregularities.

3. Cut two dadoes *, each the thickness of the jambs. The jambs too, should be made from $^5/_4''$ thick lumber, so the dadoes will be about $1^3/_{16}''$ wide—but measure your wood, for the thickness of nominal $^5/_4''$ lumber varies from lumberyard to lumberyard, and you want a snug joint.

Make the first dado (actually a rabbet) at the end you want to hinge the sash. If the framing stud on this side is straight and plumb you will make the window extra strong by fixing the jamb with the hinges to it.

To make a dado mark the edges of it carefully first and then make several saw-cuts across the board, as shown at "a", and then chisel away the dado making the bottom as smooth as possible.

SAWCUTS

'a'

CHISEL

MAKING A DADO
& RABBET

A circular saw is easiest if you can set the depth of the blade (or the height of a table saw blade). (A "dado head set"—a special combination of blades for power saws—is easiest and quickest, but not really worth the time involved in setting it up if you only have one or two to cut.)

Pre-electric carpenters had planes with irons (blades) of varying widths which could be set to the required depth. However, even they most usually simply used a back saw and a chisel.

4. When the head of the frame is ready, the two jambs must be cut, and dadoed to receive the sill.

To allow water to run off, the sill should slope downwards toward the outside at about an angle of 15°. For a close fit when shut, the bottom of the sash should also be trimmed to a 15° angle.

SHOWING ANGLE
OF SILL & BOTTOM
OF SASH

GLASS
SASH
SILL
15°

Use the bevel square set at 15°
to mark all the cuts involving
this slope.

BEVEL SQUARE

As the window is to open outwards the sash is hinged to the outside edge of the jamb. So measure in from the outside edge of the jamb the thickness of the sash and draw a line parallel to the edge on the jamb.

OUTSIDE EDGE
OF JAMB

SASH

LINE PARALLEL TO EDGE,
THE THICKNESS OF THE
SASH

5. Fit the jamb into the dado in the head and measure off the height of the sash along this line, plus ¼″ for clearance of the sash while it is being opened and closed. Draw a line at 15° across the jamb to intersect this point and you have the top edge of the dado to receive the sill, as shown.

6. Measure the exact thickness of the sill—it may be made from ⁵/₄″, but better windows usually use 2″ stock—and mark off this thickness below the first line and cut the dado as for the head. Do this for both jambs and you have:

7. Cut off the bottom of the jambs so that the frame will fit easily into the rough

**THE DADO
MOLDING PLANE**

End View of a Left-
Handed Dado Plane

opening (with ½" or so to spare—so that one side or the other may be shimmed up if the opening is not perfectly square).

8. Now cut the sill as shown:

THE SILL

9. The back of the sill must now be cut at a 15° angle to be vertical, and a groove cut under the front edge to act as a drip edge. This groove is most easily cut by running the electric saw along, ¼" in from the edge, with the blade set ¼" deep.

10. Now all four sides of the frame are complete and the whole thing should be nailed together and placed in the rough opening, taking care to see that it is as square as possible—or the sash will not fit.

THE FINISHED FRAME

The frame is held in place by nailing the outside trim to the edges of the frame and to the studs comprising the rough opening (through the sheathing). But first, the building paper should come to the edge of the frame as explained in chapter 3.

MAKING THE TRIM

Cut and nail the two side pieces first—remembering to cut the bottom edges at 15°—so that the bottom edge rests closely on the sill and the top edge extends ¼" above the bottom of the head.

OUTSIDE SIDE TRIM

SILL

Bottom cut at 15°

Width — according to taste, in older buildings usually ⁵⁄₄" x 6", in new buildings often 1" x 4", but in any event wide enough to span the distance between the edge of the frame and the stud forming the side of the rough opening.

OUTSIDE TRIM

STUD

HEAD

JAMB

Then the top piece (architrave) is cut, its length being the distance from the outside edge of one trim to the other. On the top edge of this is nailed a piece of drip cap the same length.

Nail Drip Cap with Finish Nails.

FINISHED TRIM OUTSIDE SHOWING NAIL-ING—WHICH SHOULD BE SET AND FILLED AS IS THE SIDING (see chapter 4).

The inside trims, fitted after the walls are finished, are fitted in the same order, with the exception of the drip cap, and the addition of two extra pieces called the stool, and, inside, level, sill, and the apron—essentially the bottom piece of trim which also helps support the stool.

The stool is fitted first, the sides being extended, like the sides of the sill, to be at least as wide as the side pieces of trim.

Then the apron is cut the same length (or 1″ shorter) and nailed firmly under the stool. Finally the side pieces and the top piece are cut and nailed. The inside trim is more usually 1″ x 4″ and so need only be nailed with 8d. finish nails. Most lumberyards also carry interior window casing to be used as trim. A common variety is the Clamshell pattern:

This is also used to trim the insides of door frames. The corners should be mitered.

With the frame built, and the trim holding it square and secure, the next step is
to hang the window. Remember the sash should fit into the opening with a little
clearance (⅛″) all round, and that the bottom should be beveled to match the
angle of the sill slope. Also, the inside edge of the side opposite the hinges should
be beveled slightly to allow the window to close and not leave too big a gap.

Using a chisel, mortise out the hinges in the edge of the sash so that the face of
the hinge is flush.

1. Mark the position of the hinges on the edge of the sash. Do not lay the hinge over the tenons of the rails.

2. Make vertical cuts with the chisel along the marks you have made.

3. Cut away the wood with the chisel.

* Always leave some wood at "X", rather than cutting the mortise all the way
across the edge, it makes the hinge stronger to have three sides to bear against
instead of two.

This hinge can only bear on 2 sides

With both hinges screwed to the sash, hold that sash in the frame and mark the position of the hinges on the frame—the outside of the sash being flush with the outside edge of the frame—cut out the hinge mortises in the frame, and screw everything together. To make life easier, it is possible to buy "loose pin" butts (hinges that come apart). Using this kind you can screw both parts of the hinge to the sash and the frame separately.

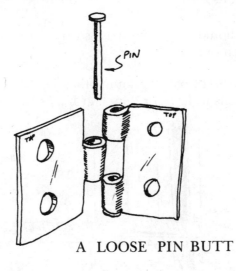

A LOOSE PIN BUTT

When the sash is hung, the only job that remains is to make the stop. The stop is the strip which runs around the inside of the frame, and against which the window closes. If you have built a stool, this serves as the bottom stop. Stop molding may be bought at lumberyards, or for something more substantial you may use some 1″ x 2″.

2. Doors.

Much of what has been said about windows can be said about doors. They too may be bought as units, complete with frame, casing, and sill; or old doors may be obtained, much more cheaply, and be framed in essentially the same manner as casement windows.

Some important points and differences to note are:

1. Exterior doors should open inwards, so that storm doors and screen doors may be hung to open outwards.

2. Sills should be made of oak (or some other HARD wood) which are available in standard dimensions to fit most doors, at lumberyards.

DETAIL OF DOOR SILL

3. Interior doors may be hung on which ever side, and to open inwards or outwards as convenience dictates. They are generally lighter and smaller than exterior doors and are trimmed the same on both sides.

4. Full length doors are usually hung with three hinges to prevent warping and sagging.

SOME DIFFERENT COMMON SIZES AND DESIGNS OF DOORS

3. Ceilings and Walls.

Ceilings and walls may be finished in a number of different ways, including plastering, panelling with wood or plywood, using various composition boards, or most commonly using gypsum board which may be either painted or papered.

1. Plastering is still one of the best ways of finishing quality houses although it is relatively expensive and requires a lot of skill—in fact, proper plastering is a trade in itself.

2. Plywood is made for interior use in a large variety of veneers and patterns. It too is very expensive but has the advantage of being very quickly applied compared with plastering which may require long periods to cure (dry). It is usually made to imitate vertical wood panelling and is usually applied vertically (on the walls). Care must be taken to ensure that all sheets are plumb and fitted tightly together, and that there is adequate nailing along all edges.

3. Wood panelling requires a high level of carpentry skill although it is relatively straightforward to cover wall surfaces with matched boards, and tongue and grooved knotty pine panelling is very popular.

SECTION OF WOOD WALL PANELLING AROUND A FIREPLACE

TONGUE & GROOVED KNOTTY PINE

"MATCHED" BOARDS

4. Gypsum board—more usually called Sheetrock, and sometimes plasterboard— is a material made in various thicknesses, and sheets 4′ x 8′, 4′ x 10′ and 4′ x 12′, consisting of a gypsum filler sandwiched between layers of paper. The edges are recessed to receive the joint compound which covers the edges.

Assuming the walls are framed with studs 16″ on center, ⅜″ thick sheets may be used, although ½″ thick sheets are better insulation, more fireproof, more rigid and less likely to bend.

If the whole interior is to be sheetrocked, the ceilings should be done first, nailing every 6″ to every framing member (second floor joists or rafters), with all joints centered over wood—as with sheets of plywood. Use 5d. cement-coated nails, or special Sheetrock nails which have flat heads and rings on the shanks to prevent them from pulling out. Or use two nails at a time, driven in at opposing angles.

Hammer the nails in just below the surface so that the resulting indentation may be filled with spackle (joint compound) and then sanded smooth.

Joint compound is most economically bought in 5 gallon cans, although it is possible to buy it in ½ pint cans.

When sheets must be cut, draw a straight line, or snap a chalk line, and score along this line with a mat knife, then fold the Sheetrock away from the cut and make another cut in the V thus formed.

After the ceiling has been covered, do the walls, using the sheets vertically or horizontally, which ever way involves least cutting and fewest joints. Try to keep the joints tight, especially in the corners, but do not worry about the edge at the floor, since the baseboard covers this.

AN OUTSIDE CORNER,
SHOWING USE OF
METAL CORNER STRIPS

When all the sheets are nailed in place the nail holes must be spackled and the joints taped.

First spread a layer of spackle along the joint, then press the tape over the crack and spread some more spackle over the whole, using a broad knife to feather the edges.

Allow this to dry, at least 24 hrs., sand smooth and repeat until the joint is perfectly smooth.

When taping in the corners, fold the tape first so that it fits more easily into the corner.

4. Floors.

This is the last to be done, after the walls are finished, because the baseboard, which runs around the bottom of the wall, sits on top of the finish floor.

The first thing to ensure is that the subfloor is well nailed, level and clean. Then a layer of building paper is applied over the whole surface; this prevents dust passing through the floor and helps insulate the room from the crawl space or basement below.

Wood flooring is usually matched—grooved—in some way so that the boards fit tightly into one another. Hardwood floors such as maple and oak are often made with short narrow strips, side and end matched—i.e., tongue and grooved on all four sides.

Other hardwoods such as beech, birch, walnut, ash, and hickory are also used, but more rarely. Hardwood floors are best since they wear longer, but pine, fir and hemlock—classed as softwoods—are also common flooring materials since they are considerably cheaper. These are also manufactured in matched, narrow pieces, but wider boards are more common. Indeed, in older houses it is not uncommon to find floorboards made of pine up to 18″ in width.

Pine is still among the cheapest floorings, and random width pine boards (6″, 8″ and 10″ wide) may be bought directly from sawmills, milled on one side, and tongue and grooved, much cheaper than packaged hardwood floors.

However, the wider the board, the more subject it is to expansion and contraction through changes in the moisture content, and this can result in unsightly gaps between floorboards.

Thus, one of the most important elements in obtaining lumber for flooring is being sure that the wood is properly dried. Green, unseasoned wood will shrink in a few months, often by a surprising amount.

The direction the floorboards should run may be determined by any, or ideally but rarely all, of the following:

1. The boards should lie at right angles to the joists.

2. The boards should lie at right angles to the subfloor—or at 45° if the subfloor has been laid diagonally.

3. The boards often look best if laid lengthwise along the room.

Having decided which way the boards are to run, start by placing the grooved edge against one wall and nailing through the top and tongue as shown, preferably into a joist.

It will make it a lot easier to nail into the joists if you mark with chalk where they are on the building paper as you lay it down.

If you want to avoid a squeaky floor, use nails long enough to penetrate the tongue of the board, the paper, the subfloor and the joist below, as shown on the previous page.

To avoid damaging the edges of the boards when driving the nails, use a nailset as shown. However, leaving a fraction of the nail projecting provides an added grip for the next board.

In nailing subsequent boards—be they the narrow strips or wide boards—make sure that all butt joints are well staggered.

All boards should be driven up tightly against the preceding board, using a scrap piece of flooring as a driving block, if necessary.

Crooked boards may have to be wedged up tightly and stood upon while being nailed in order to hold them in place; otherwise the floor may be out of alignment by the time the opposite wall is reached.

The secret of getting the last few boards down tightly lies in not nailing them! Fit them together, buckled, and then press them into place by standing on them.

When the floor is fully laid the door trim should be made, fitting snugly to the floor, and then all thresholds and saddles should be nailed in place where different floors meet in doorways.

The baseboard is the last piece of trim to be made. This may be anything from a small piece of 1" x 2" to an elegantly molded baseboard as much as 12" high.

1" x 2"

MOLDED BASEBOARD

TWO TYPES OF BASEBOARD

Since floors may not be absolutely level, a piece of ¼ round or cove molding, is often applied to the base of the baseboard to conceal any cracks left by the unevenness of the floor.

BASEBOARD NAILED TO THE STUDS, SET & FILLED.

Nail the molding to the floor – not to the baseboard. If the baseboard shrinks the molding stays tight to the floor!

¼ round MOLDING

FINISH FLOOR

BIBLIOGRAPHY

Hodgson, Fred T. MODERN CARPENTRY: A PRACTICAL MANUAL. Chicago: Frederick J. Drake & Co., 1909
An old, but excellent book on interior and exterior trim with detailed working drawings of doors, windows, cornices and staircases.

ARCHITECTURAL GRAPHIC STANDARDS (see bibliography at end of chapter 1.)

THE MODERN CARPENTER JOINER AND CABINET MAKER (see bibliography at end of chapter 2.)

CARPENTERS AND BUILDERS LIBRARY (see bibliography at end of chapter 1.)

APPENDIX

ESSENTIAL RED TAPE

Even someone already owning their own land is unlikely to be allowed to build willy-nilly without at least some red tape involved. So for those people, and others who do not even own land at all, this appendix is written. It covers briefly the main legal obstacles which will be encountered by the house builder.

Firstly, in securing land, there are TITLE SEARCHES, SURVEYS, and DEEDS to be made. Then there may be BUILDING CODES and ZONING LAWS to be considered, BUILDING PERMITS to be applied for, and HEALTH CERTIFICATES and CERTIFICATES OF OCCUPANCY to be obtained. Finally, on the financial side, there are LOANS, MORTGAGES, INSURANCES, ASSESSMENTS and TAXES to work out.

The Land

Becoming a land owner involves a little more than merely handing over some money and receiving a deed. Of course, circumstances vary, but the process is basically as follows:

1. Engage a lawyer, for there is a lot of paperwork to be done, most of it legally complicated.

2. A survey of the land involved is made, preferably by a licensed surveyor, sometimes at the buyer's expense, sometimes the seller's, or sometimes shared.

3. The lawyer will make a title search to discover that there are no liens against the property, no taxes outstanding and what, if any, restrictions exist as to the use of the land.

4. Then a deed for the land is drawn up, and sometimes a contract covering the terms of the sale as well. Deeds vary from weak—"Quit Claim Deeds"—which merely divest the grantor (the party selling the land) of all claim to the land, to strong—"Warranty Deeds"—which assure the grantee (the party buying the land) of full legal possession and inurement from all "encumbrances."

5. Finally, with much stamping and signing of papers, the deed is filed with the county clerk, or his equivalent.

A TRANSIT.. for SURVEYING

The Building

When the land is yours you may start to build, but you should be aware of the following possible restrictions and requirements—in fact, you should investigate these when you are considering buying the land, or you may find—after you have bought your future estate—that the local government forbids three-story thatched towers, or whatever you were planning to build.

1. Zoning Laws.

Many areas have zoning laws which govern the amount of land on which a house may be built, how near it may be built to the boundaries, what materials may be used, and many other aspects of building. Most agencies however may be approached for "variances," but this is something a lawyer is useful for.

2. Building Codes.

There may be a variety of building codes in force, ranging from state to local, which must be complied with. These sometimes set detailed standards for construction. Some areas require plumbing to be done only by licensed plumbers, and almost no power company will connect electricity without an inspection. Copies of applicable codes may usually be obtained from Town Halls or County Office Buildings.

3. Building Permits.

Some areas require that you obtain a building permit before construction may begin. This is generally to ensure that local building codes and/or zoning laws are being complied with. Where building permits are required it is also often necessary to apply for Certificates of Occupancy when the building is completed.

4. Health Certificates.

Submission of sewage disposal plans and water supply details is often required at the county level, and sometimes at the town or village level. Inspections may be made and tests conducted to see if everything satisfies local sanitation requirements.

All of the above may be readily discovered by application at local government offices, and should be thoroughly investigated *before* you start to build.

The Money

Money is needed to build the house and, just as important, to pay taxes on it after it is complete. How the money is raised to build depends on you, but the taxes are established, and you should be aware of their extent before you start.

The land is usually bought outright from the seller, and if necessary financed by a **PERSONAL LOAN.** This is something either your lawyer, or the broker managing the sale, will be able to advise you on.

MORTGAGES are usually only given on buildings already existing, and should not be confused with **BUILDING LOANS,** which is money the bank makes available to build with. This may be an outright payment of the amount considered necessary to complete the house, or it may be made in installments at different stages of construction—for example, one third for the foundation, one third for the rough framing and sewage system, etc.

Yet another way is to build part of the house with a loan or cash and then apply for a mortgage on what is already built—and use this money to complete the house.

Whichever way you finance the building, read the small print and understand the terms of the loans and mortgages, for there are many different types, and they may not all be suitable in the long run.

As soon as you own land—from the moment the deed is filed—you are liable for property taxes. As soon as you "improve" the land—for example, build a house on it—you supposedly increase its value, and will usually be taxed more. This is all ascertained by a process called **ASSESSMENT.** The assessors determine how much you will pay by considering how much you paid, what the house is worth, and what the local **TAX RATE** is. So while it helps to know in advance what the tax rate for your area is, it won't give you much idea of how much your taxes will be unless you also know the value of your proposed house.

There are a variety of taxes which you may have to pay, depending on locality. Taxes may be levied by the **TOWNSHIP, TOWN** or **VILLAGE,** and the **COUNTY**—the respective offices of which will give you all the information you need.

Then there are a number of special taxes which may apply, including **SCHOOL TAX, WATER TAX,** and **SEWAGE TAX.** These are likely to be administered by separate bodies, and the districts they control may or may not overlap. Once again, your local town offices will tell you what you are liable for—but find out in advance—if you don't pay, liens may be put on your house, mortgage applications denied, and your house may be auctioned off to pay the back taxes.

POSTSCRIPT

With the outside complete, the wiring, plumbing, insulation, and heating installed, the walls and ceilings finished, the floors laid, and the trim work complete, the house is virtually finished. While theoretically possible, it is rarely that anyone who builds his own house is ever able to say "finished!", for improvements and additions are constant. Consequently, what has been explained in this book is merely the basic structure of a house.

Subjects such as chimney building, staircase making and cabinetry, etc., would require volumes to themselves. Nevertheless, the subjects covered have been made as clear and as complete as possible.

But new developments and techniques occur continuously, and I would welcome any suggestions which might improve the usefulness of this book.

Illustrated
Interior Carpentry

For Heide Duggal

CONTENTS

INTRODUCTION

Encouraged by the success with which my earlier book ILLUSTRATED HOUSE-BUILDING has met, I have written this book to follow on and, to a certain degree, to complete many of the topics necessarily given only scant attention in the earlier work.

The present book is, however, organized along different lines and need not be read from beginning to end, but may be dipped into here and there as the need dictates. There is a certain logic to the order in which the various subjects are treated, but so many things must be done in overlapping stages that it would be impossible to describe coherently the finishing of a house in strict chronological order, and the various subjects are therefore treated separately, one at a time.

It should be borne in mind that the main purpose of this book, like that of its predecessor ILLUSTRATED HOUSEBUILDING, is to enable the average person to build and complete a house. It is not, therefore, an exhaustive treatise on all aspects of woodworking and joinery. Many things are left out because they are beyond the scope of what is required for a small house.

The main requisite has been that there be enough information for the layman to build well and with a choice of alternatives. Those who would become professional carpenters, joiners, or architects must certainly know what is written here, but they will also have to know much more if they are to become fully competent in their fields.

Nevertheless, I would like to emphasize that I have in no way pandered to the weekend-dabble or half-interested do-it-yourselfer. The information presented here is, I hope, completely "professional." If anything, I have erred on the side of craftsmanship rather than on the side of expediency. Indeed, many shoddy tricks and short cuts are to be met within so-called "professionally built" houses today. It is a shame that with so many new and wonderful materials at our disposal—such as thermopane, fiberglass insulation, Formica, and even sheetrock and plywood—that so little "craftsmanship" is in evidence in new buildings. There are, of course, exceptions, but so much of the work covered in this book, namely the millwork, finish carpentry, and joinery, that goes on in even high-cost dwellings is shoddy in extreme compared to the same work of even fifty years ago.

It is not only the cost—in terms of money and time—of our shelter that is important, but also the beauty and craftsmanship with which we surround ourselves. For these things, despite the press of financial considerations, are ultimately more important.

And for the reader of this book there is something else that is important: a door, for example, though not mechanically perfect, is worth infinitely more if we have, with intelligence and application, made it ourselves rather than bought a possibly more expensive installation from a "home components fabricator."

Finally, it is assumed that the reader will have a passing acquaintance with the basic woodworking skills. However, the most important requirements are integrity and patience, for, though skill and technique may come with practice and experience, little of value will ever be achieved if we do not care.

Graham Blackburn

DIMENSIONS

The subject of dimensions is at the moment somewhat confusing, firstly, because of the system of classifying milled lumber in terms of sawmill cuts (that is to say, although the sawmill may cut an exact 2" x 4", by the time the wood has been seasoned, dried, and milled, it may measure anything from 1½" x 3½" to 1-11/16" x 3-11/16" and yet still be called a 2" x 4"); and secondly, because of the changeover to the metric system, which is imminent in America and already under way in Britain.

Ultimately, the adoption of the metric system will have simplified matters greatly; indeed, in Britain new standards are being laid down which are a vast improvement over the old "imperial" system of inches and feet. Therefore, I have avoided the use of actual measurements where not strictly necessary, but where they occur, bear in mind that lumber measurements are "nominal" and other measurements are "standard" American.

In general, it is the proportions which are important, and although a millimeter may be more convenient than an inch, in the long run it will matter little what the proportional units were called at the time of construction.

A NOTE ON THE TITLE OF THIS BOOK

CARPENTRY AND JOINERY

CARPENTER: a workman who shapes and assembles *structural* woodwork, especially in the construction of buildings.

JOINER: one who does the woodwork (as doors or stairs) necessary for the *finishing* of buildings.

WEBSTER'S THIRD NEW INTERNATIONAL DICTIONARY

CARPENTER: one who does the framework of houses . . . as opposed to a joiner.

JOINER: a worker in wood who does lighter and more ornamental work than that of a carpenter.

THE OXFORD UNIVERSITY DICTIONARY

According to the dictionary definitions, this book should be properly entitled "Illustrated Joinery"; however, I have chosen to call it "Illustrated Interior Carpentry" for the following reasons:

Whereas the dictionary distinction between "carpenter" and "joiner" was commonly observed in years past, there are few people now who would call for a "joiner" when needing "joinery" work; rather would they call for a "carpenter" and think of the work discussed in this book as "carpentry"—or at most "finish" or "trim" carpentry. The "carpenter" of yesteryear is now referred to, in America at least, as a "framer."

Although some may object to this apparent semantic inconsistency, it should be pointed out that regardless of dictionaries or pedants, it is common usage which is the ultimate arbiter in questions of meanings. We must accept changes of meanings as part of the natural growth of language—after all, as many dictionaries will evidence, many, many words began with meanings quite different from their present ones, including "carpentry", which orginally meant "carriage-making"!

JOINERY IS A BRANCH OF CIVIL ARCHITECTURE, AND CONSISTS OF THE ART OF FRAMING OR JOINING TOGETHER WOOD FOR INTERNAL AND EXTERNAL FINISHINGS OF HOUSES . . . HENCE JOINERY REQUIRES MUCH MORE ACCURATE AND NICE WORKMANSHIP THAN CARPENTRY . . .

PETER NICHOLSON   1812

CHAPTER ONE
DOORS

Most doors may be classified as either exterior doors or interior doors. Exterior doors include front entrance doors, back entrance doors, and French windows. Interior doors include doors between rooms and closet doors.

Aside from the fact that exterior doors are usually larger and thicker than interior doors, both types share a variety of designs. Some of these are listed below.

1. LEDGED AND BRACED DOORS

Sometimes known as "batten doors" or "country-style doors," these consist of vertical boards, usually tongued and grooved together, with ledges and braces on the reverse side. Some typical examples are illustrated on the next page.

LEDGE

BRACE

TEE HINGE

BRACES INSET
IN LEDGES

BACK

FRONT

**VARIOUS DESIGNS FOR
LEDGED AND BRACED DOORS**

SINGLE
BRACE

TONGUE
GROOVE

**SHOWING THE TONGUE AND GROOVING
IN THE VERTICAL BOARDS**

2. FRAMED LEDGED AND BRACED DOORS

Framed ledged and braced doors are a more sophisticated version of ledged and braced doors. They consist of a mortised and tenoned outer frame with a sheeting of tongue and groove matched boards, ledged and braced as above. "Matched" means that the ends, as well as the sides, are tongued and grooved.

3. BEAD AND BUTT PANELED DOORS

Bead and butt paneled doors are flush panel doors, more commonly used in Britain than in America for rear entrances. The panels are tongued into the framing, being first beaded on their vertical edges.

4. PANELED DOORS

Paneled doors consist of a frame made of stiles, rails, and muntins, with panels grooved into the framing. Exterior paneled doors very often have the top, or frieze panels, made out of glass. The nimber of panels is variable and ways of fixing the panels are numerous.

TOP RAIL

FRIEZE PANEL

STILE

MUNTIN

LOCK RAIL

BOTTOM RAIL

"MALTESE CROSS"

GLASS

VARIETIES OF PANELING

PANELS   STILES

STUCK MOULD

PLANTED MOULD

SINGLE RAISED PANELS

BOLECTION MOULDS

FRAMED BOLECTION MOULD

DOUBLE RAISED PANEL

TRADITIONAL RAISED PANEL DOOR

DIFFERENT WAYS OF FIXING PANELS

5. GLAZED DOORS

Glazed doors may be fully glazed, such as French windows, or half glazed. The door may be glazed with putty or glazing compound, or fitted with wooden beads. (Sliding glass doors are discussed in Chapter Two.)

HALF GLAZED   FULLY GLAZED

6. INTERIOR PANELED DOORS

Interior paneled doors are usually thinner and narrower than exterior paneled doors. Two typical interior designs are shown below.

7. FLUSH DOORS

Flush doors consist of thin plywood faces covering a wooden frame with a solid or hollow core. The plywood faces are made from a variety of woods, including birch, oak; gum, and mahogany. Even though they are called "flush," these doors are sometimes decorated with false panels and applied mouldings.

8. PREHUNG THERMAL DOORS

Prehung doors are complete, factory-made units, prehung and often prefinished in their own frames. They are relatively easy to install, eliminating much of the traditional carpentry associated with hanging and installing doors. Unfortunately, many of the designs are imitative of older styles and the fake panels and applied mouldings give these units a strangely insubstantial look. Their main advantage lies in the fact that they often use insulating glass and "thermal exterior cores" and have been precision-engineered to eliminate drafts, weather, and dust infiltration.

9. MISCELLANEOUS DOORS

By this group I mean to include sliding doors, folding doors, revolving doors, lowered doors, and other novelty doors. Most of these, however, are types by virtue of their fitting rather than their intrinsic design.

SOUTH DOOR OF ST. HELEN'S CHURCH
BISHOPSGATE · LONDON

CONSTRUCTION

1. LEDGED AND BRACED DOORS

Doors of this kind are sometimes made without the diagonal pieces, called braces (which are, however, in reality not "braces" but "struts," designed to transmit the weight of the door to the inner ends of the middle and bottom ledges, and so prevent the dropping of the "nose" or free end of the door), and, as such, are properly known as "ledged doors," but this practice is inadvisable, since the braces also help greatly in preventing the door from warping, a very common fault in plain ledged doors.

LEDGED DOOR   BRACED AND LEDGED DOOR

The size of the lumber used and the finish size of the door will depend upon what is available, your own preferences, and the size of the opening into which the door is to fit. Suffice it here to point out that doors for outbuildings need to be stouter than interior doors, and while 1" stuff* is sufficient for the latter, you might use 2" stuff** for the former.

*25 mm—this is the approximate metric equivalent, not yet a standard.
**50 mm—ditto.

The first step is to butt together the edges of the battens (these are the vertical pieces), which may be square-edged boards, but preferably will be tongued and grooved (sometimes referred to simply as T and G).

SQUARE-EDGED BOARD

TONGUED AND GROOVED BOARD (T&G)

The battens should be a little longer than the required height of the door, and, when tightly together, a little wider than the finish width of the door. Thus all edges may be sawn square at one time, and the tongue on one side and the groove on the other be removed.

DOTTED LINE REPRESENTS FINISH SIZE

Unless you are using really well-dried wood, it is liable to shrink somewhat, so it is important that, initially at least, the battens be fitted tightly together. In good class work the edges are painted; this makes the door more weatherproof. The battens are held together by the ledges, which may be made of the same tongued and grooved material — with the edges sawn off as below.

The ledges are screwed into the outside battens and nailed to the inside battens. To hold the battens tightly together while the ledges are being fixed, you may either nail blocks to the floor and insert wedges, as shown, or simply use bar or pipe clamps.

The method of screwing and nailing the ledges is illustrated below.

LEDGES SCREWED TO OUTSIDE BATTENS FROM BACK

BACK

USE THREE OR FIVE NAILS

FRONT

LEDGES NAILED TO DOOR THROUGH FACE OF BATTENS

Note that the end battens, held by screws to the ledges (to prevent the door from sagging — as it might do if only nails were used), are screwed through from the back — the ledged side of the door — while the nails are driven through from the front, or face, side of the door.

The nails used should be 1/4" or so longer than the combined thickness of the ledge and the battens, so that after having been driven through, the ends may be clinched over, using a nail set.

Depending on how the door is to fit in its frame — which will be discussed later under the heading **INSTALLATION** — the ledges may or may not extend the full width of the door. This is readily understood from the illustration below.

A   door opening outwards, hinges fixed to face of door
B   door opening inwards, hinges fixed to back of battens
C   door opening inwards, hinges fixed to ledges
D   door opening inwards, hinges fixed to ledges, frame
     rabbeted to depth of battens, then blocked out

The ledges should not be more than 3" or so from the top and the bottom of the finished door, or the ends of the battens may suffer damage when the door is in use.

Furthermore, if the braces are to be notched into the ledges rather than simply butted, the notches must be cut in the ledges before they are fixed to the door! So bear all this in mind before beginning to nail.

BRACE BUTTED AGAINST LEDGE   BRACE NOTCHED INTO LEDGE

Exactly where the brace meets the ledge is a matter of design, as is whether you chamfer the edges, as in the illustration above, but remember that the braces only work if they run downwards toward the hinged side.

YES   NO

The procedure for notching is as follows: First cut the ledges to shape and fix them to the battens. The actual shape of the notch may vary considerably, as shown below.

DOTTED LINE IS AT 90° TO THE BRACE
DASHED LINE RUNS DOWN CENTER OF BRACE

When the ledges are notched and fixed to the battens, mark the ledges as at A, below. Then lay the brace over the ledge, as at B, below. Now mark the brace as at C and D, below.

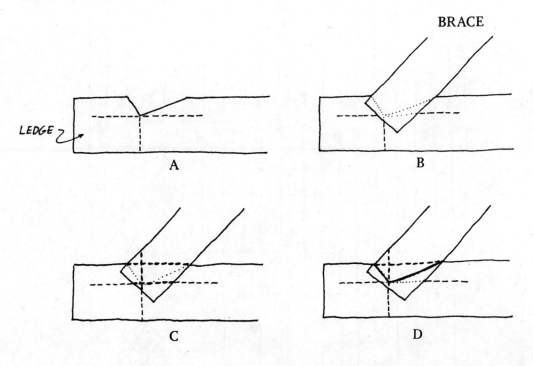

When marking the ends of the braces — whether notched or simply butted — mark both ends at the same time, lightly tacking the brace to the ledges if necessary to ensure that it doesn't slip.

After having cut the braces, nail them in place. The door is now (apart from trimming to size, which is done when it is hung, along with being fitted with its various hardware) complete.

Before the days of electrically operated, horizontally hung garage doors, ledged and braced doors were also much used for situations where doors larger than normal interior doors were needed, such as the stable doors illustrated below.

2. PANELED DOORS

Together with flush doors, whose construction will not be discussed, since they are more suited to factory manufacture than being made "on the site," paneled doors comprise the most frequently used type of interior and exterior doors.

The variations in design are almost endless. They may be plain, chamfered, beaded, or moulded on one or both sides, and the panels themselves may be worked separately and fixed on with wooden pegs or nails (technically known as "planted"), or worked on the solid (known as "stuck"). Needless to say, the overall shape of the door may vary too; the heads of the doors may be square or arched, and the panels themselves may not always be rectangular.

**DOUBLE ENTRANCE DOORS WITH ELLIPTICAL FANLIGHT AND
ROUND CENTER PANEL**

In the framing of doors, as in other framing, the vertical pieces are known as "stiles" and the horizontal pieces "rails." Any intermediate vertical piece which is tenoned into mortises formed in the rails is called a muntin (from the French "montant," meaning "mounting"). The rail next above the bottom rail is called the "lock rail." If there is another rail between the lock rail and the top rail, it is known as the "frieze rail." Similarly, the various panels are known as "frieze panels," "middle panels," and "bottom panels."

In the majority of framed doors, the top (and frieze) rails are usually the same width as the stiles ("a" in the illustration above); the bottom and lock rails usually twice as wide ("2a" above).

If the lock, or handle, is fixed at the level of the middle of the lock rail, this is usually about 3'6" (930 mm) from the bottom of the door. If the lock is fixed entirely within the stile then the lock rail may be higher or lower, as fancy dictates.

The most ordinary form of paneled door is that with four oblong panels such as illustrated below. Being devoid of any moulds or beading, it is known as a "plain" or "square-framed" door.

WEDGES

TENONS OF RAILS, BEFORE BEING WEDGED AND TRIMMED

PANEL GROOVES

STILES BEFORE BEING TRIMMED

The stiles should be cut a little longer than the height of the door and the rails somewhat longer than the width, so that the door may be uniformly trimmed after assembly (as with the ledged and braced door) and also, of course, to ensure that the mortises in the stiles are completely filled.

Each muntin must be about 4" (100 mm) longer than the adjacent panels, in order to allow for a tenon, 2" (50 mm), at each end.

Take care when making up the framework that it be of uniform thickness and finished true; that is, that each piece be perfectly square to all its edges.

The stiles and top and bottom rails must be plowed along one edge to receive the panels, and the lock rail and muntins along both edges.

(LEFT SIDE STILE NOT SHOWN FOR CLARITY'S SAKE)

The bottom of the groove in the top rail forms the bottom of the tenons at the ends, as shown below.

NOTE: HAUNCH IS 1/3 THE WIDTH OF RAIL
        TENON IS 1/2 THE DEPTH OF RAIL

Therefore, the depth of these tenons should not be much more than half the depth of the rail, for otherwise the part of the stile above the mortise may be sheared out when "wedging-up."

A haunch must be left above the tenon to fill the panel groove of the stile.

The width of the tenon is usually one-third the thickness of the door. (The panel is very often one-third the thickness of the door too, but this is variable, although usually at least one side of the panel is recessed from the frame.)

The lock rail, being of greater depth, should have two tenons at each end, as shown below.

PANEL GROOVE

TENON

LOCK RAIL

PANEL GROOVE

TENON

DETAIL AT
LOCK RAIL

Remember that the bottoms of the two panel grooves in the rail are the top and bottom limits of the tenons.

The bottom rail should also have two tenons at each end, but the bottom of the lower tenon should be at least 1½" (38 mm) from the finished bottom of the door to prevent damage in wedging-up (as with the top rails). (See illustration opposite.)

PANEL GROOVE

TENON

MID-HAUNCH

TENON

$1\frac{1}{2}"$ (38 mm)

HAUNCH

BOTTOM RAIL

DETAIL AT
BOTTOM RAIL

The tenon at each end of the muntins may be as wide as the muntins themselves, less
the depth of the panel grooves, of course, and about 2" (50 mm) long, as shown below.

2" (50mm)

TENON

PANEL GROOVE

MUNTIN

PANEL GROOVE

The mortises in the stiles must have the same width as the corresponding tenons in the rails, and the depth on the **inner** side must also equal the depth of the tenons. The top and bottom of the mortise must, however, slope upwards and downwards respectively to the outer side of the stile to allow for the insertion of the wedges.

DETAIL OF
MORTISE
IN STILE

"Wedging-up" is the last process in the framing of the door and should not be done until the panels have been fitted into position, which means, of course, that **all** the joints must have first been cut and the frame "knocked up" dry to test the fit and trueness of all the joints.

For doors thicker than 2" (50 mm), the tenons at the ends of the rails should be double. In good construction the double tenon ought always to be made at the end of the lock rail if a mortise lock is installed at this level. The tenon at this point then becomes a double pair as shown below.

PANEL GROOVE

DOUBLE TENON

MID-HAUNCH

MORTISE LOCK
FITS IN HERE

DOUBLE TENON

2"
(50mm)

LOCK RAIL

DETAIL AT
LOCK RAIL
(FOR DOORS OVER
2'' (50mm) THICK)

For hardwood doors, and other cases where it is not desired to expose the end grain of
the tenons on the edges of the stiles, fox-tail wedging is used.

MORTISE

TENON

HARDWOOD
WEDGES

FOX-TAIL WEDGING

Fox-tail wedging proceeds as follows: The mortises are cut into the stiles to within 1" (25 mm) of the opposite edge, and the tenons cut even a little shorter to permit the shoulders of the rail to butt tightly against the stile even if the wedges should fold over in driving.

The tenon for the top rail is shown below. The wedges are inserted a little way into saw cuts at the end of the tenon and the tenon is then inserted into the mortise (which must be cut to a dovetail shape) and driven in until the joint is tight.

FOX-TAIL WEDGING FOR TOP RAIL TENON

Each panel may be made from a single board (plywood is often used in mill-made doors), or from two or more pieces either plain butt-jointed and glued, or tongued and grooved and glued. If made from several pieces, the panels must afterwards be planed to a true surface.

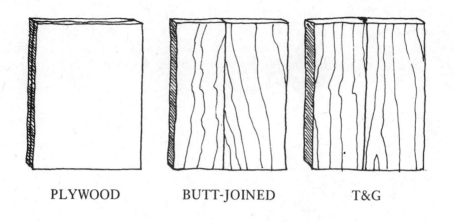

PLYWOOD   BUTT-JOINED   T&G

The most important point about the panels is that they must not be rigidly fixed in the framing, neither nailed nor tightly wedged, but must be free to move in the grooves so that in the event of shrinkage, they will not crack. This danger is less likely, of course, if the panels are made of plywood. Similarly, if mouldings are planted around the panels, they must be nailed to the framing, not to the panels, or the panels will either crack or pull the moulding away from the frame.

The panels may be quite plain or worked in a variety of ways. Sometimes the paneling is raised and sometimes recessed. Eighteenth-century paneling was almost always raised, the center of the panel being flush with the face of the stile, with the chamfer cut out of the solid wood and having a shallow square shoulder around the center (sometimes called the reserve). Any moulding was usually stuck rather than planted, as was the custom in the Middle Ages (and is again now).

STILE   PANEL

PLAIN PANEL   RAISED PANEL IN STUCK   RAISED PANEL IN
                     MOULDING (18th CENT.)   PLANTED MOULDING

Fine hardwood doors designed for interior use are often veneered over solid stock. This is because hardwoods are very expensive and have a greater tendency to twist and warp. Veneering is more suitable for the paneling and may be applied in a patterned manner.

VENEERED
PANELING

INSTALLATION

Although exterior doors, being usually larger and heavier, are set in frames more substantial and somewhat more complicated than frames for interior doors, both types have the same basic parts: a frame, consisting of lintel, jambs with stuck or planted stops, and a threshold; and architraves, usually referred to as casings, which trim the frame into the wall.

Since the lintel is technically a horizontal member over an opening (such as a doorway, window, or arch) designed to support the superincumbent weight, the piece at the top of a door frame which connects the two jambs is now usually called the head jamb, since, although "jamb" implies a vertical member (it comes from the French word for "leg"), it supports nothing but its own weight—the weight above the opening being supported by a "header" in the wooden framing.

Older construction invariably rabbeted out the jambs to provide a stop for the door, but modern construction usually makes a plain frame and then fixes a separate stop for the door—as will be explained further on.

The main difference between interior and exterior doors is the sill, which all exterior
doors must have. In general, hinged doors should open in the direction of natural entry,
especially in the case of exterior doors, which are often with a screen or storm door
(which, of course, must open outwards, contrary to the general rule).

This inward opening is more difficult to weatherproof than an outward opening and
has occasioned a variety of sills designed to shed water outwards and prevent its entering
the house. It must therefore slope downwards and outwards. The threshold may be an
integral part of the sill, as shown at A, or attached separately, as shown at B.

A   B

The sill (and threshold) should be of hardwood to better resist wear, and indeed most mill-made sills which may be bought at lumberyards are made of oak.

It is usual to place the sill between the rough opening, over the sub floor, and bring the jambs down to the sill.

If the threshold is an integral part of the sill, it must be the width of the door thickness and beveled slightly at the front to allow the front of the door to project a little, forming a drip. Also, the back of the sill should have a lip to project over the finish floor, hiding the joint.

SILL WITH
INTEGRAL
THRESHOLD

However, very often the threshold (or saddle, as it is sometimes called, because it strad-dles the joint between the two finish floors, if they be laid separately, of adjacent rooms) is fixed separately after the jambs have been installed. In this case it is cut to the width of the finished opening and should be undercoated or caulked to form a watertight seal between sill and finish floor.

SILL WITH SEPARATE THRESHOLD

Like exterior frames, interior frames may also be set on the sub floor and have the fin-ish floor fitted **around** them. This method secures the frame firmly, but it is also possi-ble to fix the frame to the finish floor. Details of sills, thresholds, or saddles may vary from house to house, but, provided you accommodate the basic requirements of slope and sealing, all will be well.

Once you have determined what will happen at the base of the opening, you may set the frame. This should be wide enough so that its outside edges are flush with the finish surfaces of both sides of the wall in which the frame is located. This enables the trim to cover the joint as shown at A, opposite. However, sometimes the outside siding is butted up against the trim, rather than running under it. In this event the frame must be flush with the outside of the *sheathing*, as shown at B, opposite.

JAMB WIDTHS FOR EXTERIOR DOORS

NOTE: For interior doors the jamb is made as at B, since there is not siding (the sheathing being another wall of sheetrock).

The rough opening should have been made large enough to accommodate the door, its frame, and an inch or so of blocking between the frame and the rough opening.

The main thing about installing the frame is that, regardless of the rough opening, the frame must be installed perfectly plumb and square. Therefore, make your frame (with the side jambs rabbeted* into the head jamb as shown below) in such a way that the head jamb will fit nicely between the studs of the rough opening, and so that there will be enough room behind the jambs to adjust for plumbness.

*The 5/4" (30 mm) stock should be used for exterior doors and good quality interior doors, but 3/4" (20 mm) stock is often used in cheaper work.

NOTE: If one of the studs of the rough opening is **perfectly** plumb, then one of the side jambs may be fixed at the end of the head jamb. In this way the side jamb may be fixed directly to the rough opening and made more secure. But it must still be squared forwards and backwards. If **both** studs are **perfectly** plumb, then fix that jamb which will carry the hinges.

If the door is perfectly level, the jambs may be of equal height, but if the floor slopes from one side of the opening to the other, one jamb will necessarily be longer than the other (in order that the head jamb may remain perfectly level). If the floor slopes backwards or forwards through the opening, the bottoms of the jambs will have to be cut accordingly.

Whatever the case may be, make sure that the head jamb is level (it is easier to fix it if it fits snugly in the rough opening), and the side jambs reach the floor—although you do have a little leeway if you are installing the frame onto the sub floor, since the finish floor will cover some of the gap.

When you are satisfied that the head jamb is level, the side jambs must be made plumb and fixed to the rough opening. One easy way of doing this is by using wedges made from shimming shingles, a bundle of which is very useful for the house under construction. After the jambs are plumb—and square—that is, they protrude from the rough opening the correct amount—on *both* sides of the opening—nail through the jambs and the wedge blocking into the studs.

If the door stop is to be applied separately, then nail the jamb at a point where the stop will cover the nail head! Also, it helps to toenail the bottom of the side jambs from both sides, as shown below.

While an integral stop is better security, since it prevents the insertion of a blade behind the stop to push back certain kinds of lock bolts, a separate stop facilitates the hanging of the door and also makes it possible to change the door's swing from one room to another if this should ever be desired. If you ever want to do this with an integrally rabbeted stop, you will have to cut the door down all around and install a separate stop on the frame.

In any event, it is usually best to hang the door at this stage and fix the stop (if it is separate) to the frame with the door in position.

If the door is new, the stiles will have to be sawn off flush. Then, having measured the width of the finished opening, plane the hinge stile perfectly smooth and square to an amount that will equal the lock stile, so that the two stiles are equal in width and there is a 1/16" (2 mm) clearance either side of the door.

The lock stile should be planed at a slight angle back to the stop to enable the inside edge of the door to clear the jamb when opened.

There should also be a **1/16" (2 mm)** clearance at the top of the door, and **1/8" (4 mm)** clearance at the bottom if there is a threshold, and maybe more if the door will have to clear a rug or carpet.

If the door is very oversize, it is best to leave as much of the bottom rail as possible, shortening the door from the top, since, if you take away too much of the bottom rail, the door will eventually fall apart. (This applies only to frame doors.)

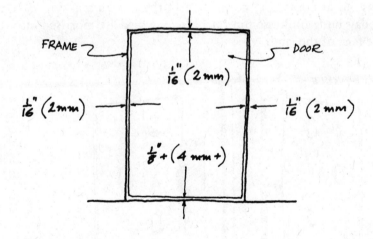

Wedge the door in the opening so that there is the correct clearance at top and bottom, but make the hinge stile butt tightly up against the hinge jamb. Three hinges are best, the lower being about 10" (250 mm) from the floor, the upper about 6" (150 mm) from the head jamb, and the middle one centered between the other two. However, if you are hanging a ledged and braced door, the hinges should be fixed to the ledges.

Hinges are as old as doors, and consequently there is an amazing variety. Most frame doors are today hung on loose pin butt hinges which are mortised into the edge of the door and the face of the jamb.

LOOSE PIN
BUTT HINGE

Most ledged and braced doors are hung on "tee" or "T" hinges, which are made in a variety of patterns and known by a number of names, some of which are illustrated below. These hinges are face mounted.

CROSS-GARNET OR T-HINGES

COMMON PRESSED HINGE

LONDON PATTERN

SCOTCH PATTERN

WROUGHT-IRON HINGE

WATER-JOINT HINGE

There are also a number of special-purpose hinges such as table-leaf hinges and invisible cabinet hinges too specialized to be discussed here. But one variety of specialty hinge deserves mention here—the rising butt hinge. This raises the door a slight amount when it is opened so that the door will close again by its own weight.

RISING BUTT
HINGE

A rising butt hinge will necessitate a slight bevel at the top of the door to allow it to clear the frame as it rises during opening.

Another advantage of the rising butt hinge is that it allows the door to clear thick carpets and yet not have a large gap at the bottom of the door when closed.

Older hinges were often made flat, whereas modern hinges are usually swaged—the difference is shown below.

FLAT   SWAGED

Swaged hinges may be mortised equally, whereas flat hinges must be offset.

FLAT HINGE

SWAGED HINGE

Assuming you are hanging a frame door with swaged butt hinges, the commonest operation, the procedure is as follows:

Mark the position of the hinge leaves on the door and the jamb, bearing in mind that if you want the door to open flat against the wall, the hinges must be set out a little so that the door will clear the casing.

The leaves of the hinges must fit flush into rabbets cut especially for them. The hinge is stronger if it has three bearing surfaces (as shown below) rather than extend right across the door.

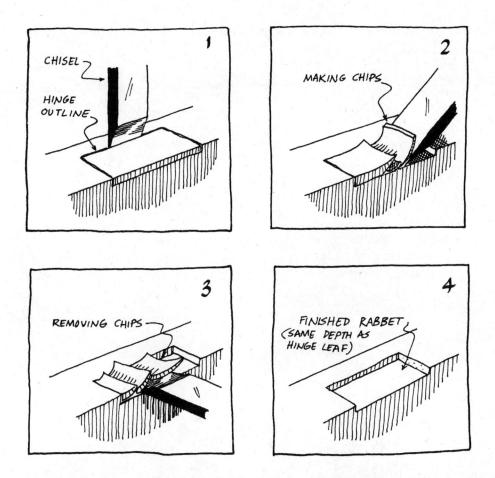

Separate the leaves of the hinges and fix each leaf with one screw only into its respective rabbet. This makes adjustment of the leaves easier when meshing the hinge knuckles.

When the door is hung, check that it opens and closes freely. If it doesn't shut all the way, you have set the hinges too deeply—in which case insert a thin piece of card behind the leaf. When you are satisfied, insert the remaining screws, but leave the pins sticking out a little in case the door must be removed again.

The door stop may now be fixed to the jambs, with the door wedged shut.

You may use a mill-made stop, which is usually moulded on one side and which should therefore be mitered at the top, or you may make up your own stop from 1" x 2" (20 mm x 50 mm) in which case it is better to butt the ends.

The door trim or casing may similarly be bought (in a variety of patterns) or made up on the job, and may be anything from a very plain board to an ornately moulded architrave complete with a cabinet head.

PLAIN CASING   ORNATE ARCHITRAVE

If you use any mill-made casing with a moulded edge, such as clamshell, you will have to miter the joint between the head casing and the side casing, but this is unfortunate, since, even if this joint is made with a spline, it almost inevitably shrinks and leaves an unsightly gap.

CLAMSHELL MOULDING

SHRINKING MITER

It is therefore better to use a plain casing and make a butt joint, adding any moulding you desire separately.

In this case, fix the side pieces first, setting them back an equal amount all around from the edge of the jambs.

The head piece may then be measured and fitted exactly.

Be careful when nailing the jamb edge of the casing not to pull the jamb out of line. Also make sure that you nail the other side of the casing into a stud.

Furthermore, when spacing the nails, be sure not to nail where the lock or striker plate will be located.

Most of the remaining hardware, such as locks, handsets, knockers, spy holes, letter slots, etc., comes in package form, usually with installation instructions and templates, and it is beyond the scope of the book to describe every type.

RABBET VERSUS REBATE

Considerable confusion exists on both sides of the Atlantic regarding the words "rabbet" and "rebate." The British talk about "rabbet" planes and "rebating," the Americans talk about "rabbeting," and "rabbets" themselves are spelled "rebate" in Britain, though commonly pronounced "rabbet."

All these words came into English from the French word "rabattre," meaning to beat down or reduce. Since the spelling "rebate" is commonly used in Britain and America to refer to a financial repayment, I have thought it useful to limit the woodworking applications of the word to the older spelling "rabbet."

Consequently, I have used "rabbet" for noun, adjective, and verb throughout this book; *e.g.*:

      a rabbet, instead of a rebate (British)
      a rabbet plane, instead of a rebate plane (rare)
      to rabbet, instead of rebate (American and British variety)

RABBET

BEECH RABBET PLANE

RABBETING

CHAPTER TWO
WINDOWS

All windows consist of two basic parts: the glazed frames, called sashes (and sometimes casements), and the frames or cases of various kinds which contain these. Windows are generally classified according to the manner in which the sash is held in the frame; these classifications may be described as follows:

1. FIXED WINDOWS
2. CASEMENT WINDOWS
3. DOUBLE HUNG WINDOWS

Before describing the construction of the various types in detail, it should be pointed out that all kinds of windows may be obtained as ready-made units from a number of manufacturers in many different shapes, styles, and sizes. They may be made of wood or metal, and most come with frame, sash, and trim assembled. Often they are glazed and have the appropriate screens, weatherstripping, and hardware in place. Furthermore, they may be made with double glass, which is much more efficient as a thermal barrier than single panes, both for keeping the house warm in winter and cool in summer.

They are, of course, much more expensive, unit for unit, than other windows, but most professional builders now prefer them because they save so much time—and so, for the contractor, so much much money. All that need be done is to order the right size in the appropriate style, place it in the rough opening, and when the inside walls are finished and the outside walls are sheathed, position the unit and secure it in place by nailing the trim or casing to the window frame and the inside and outside walls.

PREFABRICATED WINDOW INSTALLATION

1. FIXED WINDOWS

Theoretically, fixed windows are not really windows at all, since the word "window" comes from a Saxon word meaning "wind eye" and referred to a hole in the house, often the roof, through which not only light, but also air, wind, and, most important in those days, smoke could pass and fresh air enter.

The only requirement for successful construction of fixed windows is that the glazing be properly done and the sash be secure and watertight in its frame, which may usually be effected by good flashing and caulking.

FIXED WINDOW

2. CASEMENT WINDOWS

Casement windows have sashes which may be hung to swing inwards or outwards, hinged from the top (called awning sash), from the bottom (called hopper sash), or from the sides. The window may consist of one sash or a double sash, or even two sashes and a fixed central sash (the last arrangement being applicable to double hung windows also).

Casement windows have the advantage of being able to be opened completely—and of catching a parallel breeze and slanting it into the room.

If they open inwards, as is usual in Europe, the fixing of screens and storm sashes is facilitated, and both sides of the glass may be cleaned from within the room. If they open outwards, as is more usual in Britain and America, screens and shutters must be fixed on the inside—which makes it difficult to open or close the window without special hardware—which so often gets stuck! However, it is easier to make outward-opening casement windows watertight, particularly against driving rain and snow.

CASEMENT WINDOW

3. DOUBLE HUNG WINDOWS

The double hung window consists of two sashes which slide past one another, usually vertically. These windows have some advantages and some disadvantages. The advantages are that screens and storm sash can be located on the outside without interfering with the operation of the window, and ventilators and air conditioners can be placed easily in the window. The disadvantages are that only one-half of the window area may be opened at any one time, and that construction is a little more involved than for casement windows.

DOUBLE HUNG WINDOW

NOTE: This type of window is often confusingly referred to as a "sash" window—all windows have sashes! What is really meant is a window, the sash of which is balanced by sash weights, which are described further on, in contradistinction to casement windows, the sashes of which are hung on hinges.

CONSTRUCTION

Factory-made window units, as mentioned before, come complete and require only to be put in place and secured there, usually by the inside and outside trim. Such convenience is, however, costly, and for the owner-builder, for whom time is not as expensive as it is for the contractor-builder, there are distinct advantages in dealing with windows differently.

One possibility is to obtain secondhand units from breakers' yards or secondhand building supply firms. It is often possible to find really handsome, well-made windows at a fraction of their cost when new. What is more difficult is to find exactly the right size or sufficient of the same sort.

A more practical approach for someone who has time, and desires to save money, and still have a well-made window, is to buy secondhand sash and make the frames. It is possible to find sash in almost any size and pattern, and providing the stiles and rails are big and strong enough, they may be hung in almost any fashion you desire.

Again, the sash is the part which holds the glass. If there are several panes of glass in the sash, it is described as a four-light, six-light, or twelve-light window, according to however many panes there are. The frame is the part that holds the sash, and includes the casing, which holds the frame in the wall.

FOUR-LIGHT
WINDOW

SASH

SIX-LIGHT
WINDOW

TWELVE-LIGHT WINDOW

1. CASEMENT WINDOWS

Having obtained appropriate sashes that will fit into the rough openings with **4" to 6"** (**100 mm to 150 mm**) space around all sides (smaller sash can be accommodated by making the rough opening smaller), first measure the width of the rough opening as shown below.

A = WIDTH OF ROUGH OPENING

FRAMING OF WALL

Next, cut a piece of **5/4"** (**30 mm**) lumber to be the head jamb of the window frame as shown below.

The length equals A—the width of the rough opening less an 1/8" (3 mm) in order that the head jamb will fit easily into the rough opening.

The width, B, equals the width of the studs, plus the thickness of the exterior sheathing and the interior finish wall, plus another 1/8" (3 mm) or so for irregularities.

SHOWING WIDTH OF HEAD JAMB IN RELATION TO ROUGH
OPENING AND INTERIOR AND EXTERIOR TRIM CASING

PARTS OF A WINDOW FRAME

In what will be the underside of the head jamb, cut two dadoes, each the thickness of the jambs.

RABBET   DADO

PLOW
(PLOUGH)

GROOVE

A DADO IS A GROOVE **ACROSS** A BOARD
A RABBET IS A GROOVE **ACROSS THE END** OF A BOARD
A PLOW IS A GROOVE **ALONG** A BOARD
A GROOVE OCCURS IN THE **EDGE** OF A BOARD

"GROOVOLOGY"

The jambs, as well as the head, should be made from 5/4" (30 mm) lumber; therefore the dadoes will be the same width as the thickness of the lumber being used. Measure this carefully, for you want a snug joint.

Make the first dado (actually a rabbet) at the end you want to hinge the sash. If the framing stud on this side is straight and plumb, you will make the window extra strong by fixing the hinge jamb directly to it.

DADO   C   RABBET

B

A

In the illustration on the previous page, C equals the width of the sash to be hung, plus a small clearance space. The dadoes should be about one-third the depth of the lumber being worked.

To make a dado, mark the edges of it carefully first, and then make several saw cuts across the board, as shown at A below, and chisel away the dado, making the bottom as smooth as possible, as shown at B below.

SAW CUTS

CHISEL

MAKING A DADO
& RABBET

A circular saw is easiest if you can set the depth of the blade (or the height of a table saw blade). A "dado head set"—a special combination of blades designed for electric saws—is easiest and quickest, but not really worth the time involved in setting it up if you only have one or two dadoes to cut.

Pre-electric carpenters had planes with irons (blades) of varying widths which could be set to the required depth. However, even they usually simply used a back (tenon) saw and a chisel.

When the head of the frame is complete, the two jambs must be cut to length and dadoed to receive the sill. The length of the jambs depends on the size of the sash and the thickness of the sill. Whatever this measurement turns out to be, add a little more so that the frame you are building will stand on the rough opening at the height you desire. This, of course, is something you will have had to have taken into account when designing the window, for everything will have affected this positioning—from the dimensions of the rough opening to the size sash you are now working with.

VARIOUS ROUGH OPENINGS WITH FRAMES IN POSITION

To allow water to run off, the sill should slope downwards and outwards at an angle of about **15 degrees**. Assuming the sash to be **hung** is going to open outwards—the commonest arrangement where English is spoken—the bottom of the sash should also be trimmed to a matching **15 degrees**, for a close fit when shut.

As the window is to open outwards, the sash is hinged to the outside edge of the jamb. Therefore measure in from the outside edge of the jamb the thickness of the sash, and draw a line parallel to the edge at this distance.

SASH

JAMB

LINE PARALLEL TO EDGE OF JAMB, THE SAME DISTANCE FROM THE FRONT OF THE JAMB AS THE SASH IS THICK

Fitting the jamb into the dado previously cut in the head, measure off the height of the sash along this line, adding 1/4" (5 mm) to allow the sash to open and close freely. Draw a line at **15 degrees** across the jamb to intersect this point—and you have the top edge of the dado to be cut to receive the sill, as shown below.

A = HEIGHT OF
   SASH + ¼" (5mm)

A

HEAD

JAMB

LINE MARKING THICKNESS OF SASH

LINE DRAWN AT 15° MARKING TOP OF SILL DADO

Now measure the exact thickness of the sill—it may be made from 5/4" (30 mm) stock, but better windows are usually made with 2" (50 mm) stock—and mark off this thickness below the first line and cut the dado as for the head. When this has been done on both jambs the frame should look as below.

HEAD

JAMB

SILL DADO

15°

ANGLE OF
SILL DADO

At this point you may have to trim the bottoms of the jambs so that the frame will fit easily into the rough opening—with a little to spare so that one side or the other may be shimmed up if the opening is not perfectly square.

LEUCADIA 77

The sill should now be cut to the pattern and dimensions shown below.

A   the distance between each dado bottom in the jambs
B   the distance between the inside faces of the jambs,
    which should equal the width of the sash plus ¼" (5 mm)
C   the width of the dado in the jamb
D   at least 2" (50 mm)
E   the same as the width of the outside trim (4"-6" (100 mm-150 mm))

The back of the sill must be cut at an angle of **15 degrees** in order to be vertical, and a groove cut in the under side of the front to act as a drip edge.

DRIP EDGE
GROOVE

BACK EDGE
CUT AT 15°

SILL SEEN FROM END

Now that all four sides have been cut, the whole thing should be nailed together and placed in the rough opening to see if it fits! When nailing take care to get the frame as square as possible, or the sash will not fit.

TESTING THE FINISHED FRAME
WITH A FRAMING SQUARE

The frame is held in place by nailing the outside trim to the edges of the frame and to the studs comprising the rough opening (through the sheathing, and a layer of building paper).

The trim is usually made and fixed to the frame before the whole is placed in the opening—that is, the outside trim, for at this stage in the building of a new house the inside walls are unlikely to be finished—you couldn't get the frame in the opening anyway if the trim were on both sides!

The procedure for making the trim is as follows. Cut and nail to the frame two side pieces first, remembering to cut the bottom edges at **15** degrees so that the slope of the sill will be matched. The top of the trim should extend a little beyond the bottom of the head—by the same amount, in fact, that the sides are set in.

The width* is a matter largely of taste. In older American buildings it is usually (5/4" x) 6"; in new buildings it is often reduced to (1"x) 4". The future metric standard may well be (30 mm x) 100 mm, but this has not yet been established in America. At any rate the trim must be wide enough to reach from jamb to stud and should equal the ear extension of the sill.

After the side pieces of trim have been fixed, the length of the top piece of trim may be accurately measured (from the outside of one side piece to the outside of the other). On the top of this is nailed a piece of drip cap—of the same length.

COMPLETED EXTERIOR TRIM (NAILS SHOULD
BE SET AND FILLED)

Examination of older buildings, especially colonial style, will reveal the variety of trim details that is possible. What has been here described is the basic technique, which may be adapted to suit the architectural style of your fancy.

As with exterior trim, interior trim is also subject to a wide variety of styles. However, in essence it is the same as the exterior trim, though usually smaller in proportions. There is, of course, no drip cap (though there may be a cabinet head—see the previous chapter) and there are usually two extra pieces not found on the outside: the stool and the apron.

The stool is fitted first, the sides being extended, like the sides of the sill, to be at least as wide as the side pieces of trim.

Then the apron is cut the same length (or 1'' (25 mm), shorter if the ends of the stool are finished in a nosing) and nailed firmly under the stool.

JAMB

SILL

STOOL

APRON

15° RABBET TO ACCOMMODATE SLOPE OF SILL

NOSING

CROSS-SECTION OF STOOL

How far the stool extends across the top of the sill can depend on a number of factors, one of the most common being the size and location of the stop—to be installed after the sash has been hung. Another factor influencing the shape of the stool would be the hinging of the sash to open inwards.

After the stool and apron are in place, the side pieces of trim are cut and nailed just as were the outside side trim; and so with the top piece also.

It should be pointed out that such trim was commonly made on the job and often consisted of moulded pieces superimposed. Nowadays the tendency is to use much simpler and smaller trim. As with door casings, trim for windows is readily obtainable in various patterns at most lumberyards.

Detail of inswinging casement window showing GLASS, SASH, STOOL, APRON, and SILL.

With the frame built, and the trim holding it securely and squarely, the next step is to hang the sash. Remember, the sash should fit into the opening with a little clearance all around, and the bottom should be beveled to match the angle of the sill's slope.

Also, as with doors, the inside edge of the side opposite the hinges should be beveled slightly to allow the window to open, and yet not leave too big a gap.

Hinging sashes is very similar to hinging doors on a smaller scale. At the risk of a certain repetition the main points to bear in mind are illustrated below for the sake of completeness.

When the hinges are screwed to the sash, hold the sash in the frame and mark the position of the hinges on the frame, the outside of the sash being flush with the outside edge of the frame. Then cut the mortises for the hinges in the frame and screw everything together. To make life considerably easier, use loose pin butt hinges so that each leaf may be affixed separately.

When the sash is hung, the only job that remains is to make the stop. The stop is the strip that runs around the inside of the frame and against which the window closes. If you have built a stool this will usually serve as the bottom stop.

STOP

COMPLETED CASEMENT WINDOW

The remaining stop, for the sides and top, may be bought or made, and fitted in the same way as door stop, discussed in the previous chapter.

STOCK MOULDING   1" x 2"   **BEADED**
                          (25 mm x 50 mm)

If you intend to fit a storm sash—for insulation—then the stop had best have square sides so that both sashes may close to it. Similarly, when fitting hardware such as handles and casement fasteners remember to make the stop wide enough to allow sufficient space between the two sashes.

2. DOUBLE HUNG WINDOWS

Double hung windows are more complicated than casement windows, but their basic construction is as follows.

The jambs (in the best type of construction) are rabbeted into two inner casing members which form a box with the rough framing in which the sash weights move up and down.

The jambs, in this case, are properly known as the yoke and the pulley stiles, as shown below.

The yoke and the pulley stiles, which are also referred to as the inner or rough casing, provide a nailing surface to the rough opening. The inside rough casing should lap the rough opening framing members about 1" (25 mm). The outside rough casing forms a blind stop for the sheathing.

The space between the rough opening and the pulley stile forms the box for the sash weights which counterbalance the sash. In better class construction this space is divided by a vertical piece of wood known as the pendulum. At the bottom of the stiles is usually a removable panel through which the weights may be retrieved should the sash cord break.

The faces of the yoke and stiles have a piece of wood dadoed into them, called a parting strip. This is removable in order that the upper sash may be taken out when necessary. The strip forms a center guide for the upper and lower sash, while the outer rough casing projects slightly beyond the stiles and yoke and so forms the outer guide. The inner guide is formed of regular window stop, which is also removable in order to allow the lower sash to be taken out from time to time.

At the top of the stiles two pulleys on each side (two for each sash) are mortised in flush with the stile.

The sill is an integral part of the frame and must slant downwards and outwards in order to shed water. It should have small steps, one at the point where the lower sash rests on the sill, and another near the outer edge to form a seat for window screens and storm sash. These steps prevent water, which drips on the sill, from being blown up under the sash.

The inside of the sill is finished as with a casement window—with stool and apron and trim. Likewise, the outside is finished with all the exterior trim, including drip cap.

Screens may be fitted as required, but it is always a good idea to install weatherstripping and storm windows in order to reduce heat loss when the building is being heated; the use of double glazing will also help keep the building cool during hot weather, and so reduce air-conditioning bills.

CHAPTER THREE
WALLS AND CEILINGS

With the exception of tiled and suspended ceilings, what may be used for walls may be used for ceilings too, and very often the same material is used for both in the same room, which is why walls and ceilings are here dealt with together in the same chapter.

In the old days there were really only two things you could do to finish the interior of a house: plaster it or panel it. With the development of new materials and new applications the list has expanded and now includes:

1. PLASTER
2. SHEETROCK
3. WOOD PANELING
4. PLYWOOD PANELING
5. TILED AND SUSPENDED CEILINGS

1. PLASTER

Barely fifty years ago plastering, to finish the interior walls and ceilings of a house, was the rule rather than the exception, but nowadays this is reversed, and although it is still possible to find an experienced plasterer, in most communities the majority of houses are finished with one or other of the "dry wall" techniques discussed further on in this chapter.

Nevertheless, I shall outline the basic preparatory procedure, since in many ways, particularly if cost is not a consideration, plaster is preferable.

Plaster requires some kind of base to which it is applied. There are three main types:

> **a. WOOD LATH**
> **b. METAL LATH**
> **c. ROCK LATH (GYPSUM BOARD)**

a. WOOD LATH   This is almost completely obsolete now but used to consist, in very old buildings, of green oak cut accordion fashion and spread apart on the framing.

A subsequent and better development was the use of thin strips of white pine, usually **1-1/2" x 3/8" (40 mm x 10 mm)** in **4' (1.2 m)** lengths (which allowed the lathing to be nailed economically to the framing, which was either **12" (305 mm)** or **16" (406 mm)** apart. The lathing is applied horizontally about **3/8" (10 mm)** apart. If the lath is dry it should be soaked in water before being applied to prevent it from drawing the water from the plaster.

LATHING PLAN

HOW PLASTER KEYS
ITSELF TO LATHS

b. METAL LATH   Expanded metal lath is much more common as a plaster base than wood lath and is much quicker to apply as it usually comes in sheets measuring **27" x 96" (686 mm x 2438 mm)**. It consists of sheet metal that has been slit and expanded to form innumerable openings into which the plaster is forced, thus keying it firmly to the metal base—which in turn is nailed securely to the framing. It is usually painted or galvanized to resist rusting.   It is easily cut with tin snips and the different pieces wired together every **12" (305 mm)** or so.

There was once a great variety of patterns available, but now the commonest is the herringbone pattern illustrated below.

SECTION OF HERRINGBONE METAL
LATH

The longitudinal ribs are set at an angle of **45°** and the cross strands are flattened. The ribs act as shelves and hold the plaster. The cross strands curl the plaster behind the lath, completely covering it.

c. ROCK LATH   The most common plaster base in use today is rock or gypsum lath. This comes in sheets measuring **16" x 48" (406 mm x 1219 mm)** and consists of two paper faces with a gypsum filler, and sometimes with a foil backing that serves as a vapor barrier. If the framing to which it is attached is the usual **16" (406 mm)** on center, then **3/8" (10 mm)** rock lath is sufficient. If the framing is **2' (50 mm)** on center, then **1/2" (13 mm)** should be used.

A better type of rock lath is perforated, which improves the bond between lath and plaster and which increases the time the plaster stays intact in a fire, for which reason many local building codes specify this kind only.

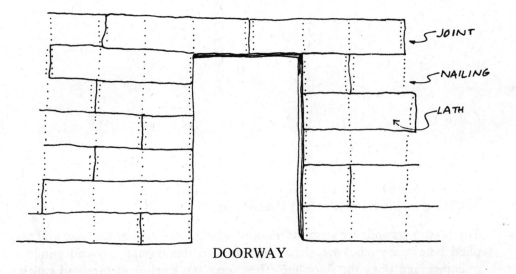

DOORWAY

HOW TO BREAK THE JOINTS BETWEEN COURSES

APPLICATION

Before applying the rock lath make sure you have adequate nailing surfaces in all corners and around all openings.

The lath is applied horizontally with the joints broken as shown.

Vertical joints should all be over studs, and sheets should not join over door and window jambs.

Nailing should be 4" (100 mm) to 5" (127 mm) on center, and 1½" (38 mm) blued and ringed lathing nails should be used.

It is often easier to fix the plaster grounds before fixing the base—although with rock lath the grounds are often fixed afterwards.

The plaster grounds are strips of wood the same thickness as the base and plaster (if applied before the base) which are attached to the framing around window and door openings, and along the floor line. They serve as a leveling surface and a plaster stop for the plaster, and along the floor line they also provide a nailing surface for the baseboard.

Strip grounds are nailed to the *inside* of the various rough openings, and are removed after plastering.

If the window and door frames are already in place, as is very often the case, then these serve as grounds—which means you must have calculated the width of the plaster and its base into the width of the door jamb. If the frames are not wide enough, you will have to fix grounds and fur the frames out before attaching the trim.

JAMB AS GROUND   NARROW JAMB REQUIRING
                                    EXTRA GROUND

To avoid cracks in the plaster caused by shrinkage of the wood framing as it dries out (in a new construction), expanded metal lath is used as reinforcement in the following places:

1. Over door and window openings as shown below.

2. Under flush ceiling beams as shown below.

3. At all exterior corners, as shown opposite, it is usual to use a metal corner bead which is plastered over and so forms a rigid corner.

The plaster, which consists of sand, lime or special plaster, and water, should be at least **1/2" (13 mm)** thick when finished.

Over wood and metal lath it is usual to apply three coats of plaster. Over rock lath the first two coats are combined and only two coats are necessary.

In three-coat work, the first coat is called the scratch coat because it is scratched before it is completely dry to ensure a good bond for the second coat, which is called the brown or leveling coat. When using rock lath as a base—which is presumably level when applied—the first two coats are combined.

The finish coat in both cases may be either rough (sand-float finish—achieved by mixing lime with sand) or smooth (putty finish—with no sand).

The mixing and application requires considerable skill; you should not expect good results the first time. There are many considerations to be borne in mind with regard to speed of drying and temperature, etc., and plastering itself is best left to a professional plasterer.

2. SHEETROCK

Sheetrock, variously referred to as drywall or gypsum wallboard, is by far the common-est material used today for walls and ceilings, and though not properly a carpenter's skill, its use is not so hard that a layman, with care, might not expect good results the first time.

It comes in sheets 4' (1.2 m) wide by 8' (2.4 m) or longer in length, and in three thick-nesses (3/8" (10 mm), 1/2" (13 mm), 5/8" (16 mm)) for use with differently spaced framing—the wider the studs are apart, the thicker should be the sheetrock. The edges of the sheets are tapered on the face side so that the joints may be filled and taped smoothly.

FILLED JOINT   TAPE   SHEETROCK

TAPERED EDGES

STUD

Professional sheetrockers use power-driven screws and nail guns, but good results may also be obtained with a regular hammer, using blued and ringed sheetrock nails like the one shown below.

SHEETROCK NAIL

RINGED FOR GREATER
HOLDING POWER

BLUED TO PREVENT RUST

Since drying of the framing may cause the nails holding the sheetrock to pop out a bit, it is best to use these ringed nails (it is even better to use the screws) and to allow the framing to dry out as much as possible before sheetrocking.

The sheets may be fixed vertically or horizontally—it is stronger horizontally, and also creates fewer joints this way—but each situation will dictate the best arrangement. It is often easier to start from the corners when covering walls, and if you are doing the ceilings too, do them first so that the ladders or scaffolding are out of the wall of the finished walls. Do not butt the sheets tightly together; leave **1/8" (3 mm)** space between sheets to allow for minor expansion changes.

SHEETROCK APPLICATION

a. **VERTICAL**
b. **HORIZONTAL**

Sheets are normally delivered in pairs, with the finish surfaces facing each other, for protection. They are heavy, especially the longer and thicker sizes, so if you have a lot of sheetrocking to do, try and have the material delivered where it will be needed—not all in one place, which might be more convenient for the delivery man.

To cut the sheets to size, or to make holes for electrical switches and outlets, score the face side first with a sheetrock knife, in order not to tear the face paper.

Then fold the sheetrock back on itself and score again in the crease. Finally, fold it the other way and it will break off.

Of course this only works if you can fold an entire flap. If you want only to cut part of the way, you must use a saw or, less messy but more effort, keep scoring with the knife until you are all the way through. Several light passes are easier than one heavy pass. Also, use a straight edge to guide the knife, or at least snap a chalk line to ensure straight cuts.

It doesn't matter so much if you tear the backing, but measure carefully—especially the position of holes—and after scoring with the sheetrock knife, use a sheetrock saw for cutting the pieces out.

METAL KEYHOLE SAW
FOR SHEETROCK

OUTLET

x'

x^2

SHEET ROCK

y' y^2

STUDS

MEASURE x' & x^2,
AND y' & y^2
CAREFULLY

HOW TO MEASURE FOR HOLES

Nailing should be every 6" (150 mm) or so on studs and round all edges. Alternatively you may space the nails 12" (300 mm) apart and then nail a second series of nails alongside the first nails (say 2" (50 mm) apart)—this helps get and keep the sheetrock tight to the studs.

6" NAILING   DOUBLE NAILING

SHEETROCK NAILING

The nails should be hammered in so that a slight dimple is left in the sheetrock—but avoid breaking the paper—in order that the depression may be filled smoothly and the nail head hidden.

SETTING THE NAILS

When all the area to be covered is sheetrocked, the "taping" begins. Like plastering, this is often something that many people, including professional builders, leave to "tapers" who do nothing else, and who are consequently very good and very fast. If you have a whole house to do, it will be quicker, cheaper, and better if done by professional tapers, but if you have only a small area, you may as well do it yourself.

All that is really needed is patience and perseverance. Firstly all nail heads are covered, using joint compound, which is most economically bought in 5 gallon (19 liter) drums,

but which may be bought in amounts as small as 1 pint (½ l.). There are various brands of joint compound which go under the different brand names. Avoid those with asbestos in them; asbestos is harmful if you inhale the dust when sanding.

To cover the nail heads, use a putty or spackle knife; anything from 2" (50 mm) to 6" (152 mm) is good.

SPACKLE KNIFE

When all the nail heads are covered, lay in a bedding coat of joint compound along all joints, and in this lay the tape—which comes in rolls; buy it with the compound.

SHEET
ROCK
TAPE

For inside corners, fold the tape first and then lay it in. When the tape is in the wet compound, smooth it down with a knife broader than the tape, taking care to maintain an even pressure, but not pressing too hard or the tape will slide out of the compound and tear.

APPLY COMPOUND

LAY IN TAPE

SMOOTH WITH KNIFE

For working in corners you may prefer to use a special "inside corner trowel."

For all exposed corners you should use an appropriate metal trim, which is simply nailed onto the sheetrock and compounded over as if it were tape.

After the bedding coat and the tape are dry, usually twenty-four hours, apply a wider, tape-covering coat and wait for that to dry. This should dry a little faster, say overnight, since you should have used less compound. Finally, apply an even wider, trowel-finished coat, using a very wide knife.

At every coating go over the exposed nail heads again, and, following the tape-covering coat and finish coat, wet-sand, using a damp sponge to avoid possibly harmful dust, to eliminate any bumps or ridges. The more careful you are when applying the compound, the less sanding you will have to do.

When taping inside corners, fold the tape well before putting it in the joint, for it could shrink when dry and end up giving you a round corner.

Lastly, don't bother to tape corners that will be hidden by moulding, such as ceiling and wall joints!

3. WOOD PANELING

Wood paneling, which for so long was the only alternative to plastering, has similarly given way to a preponderance of plywood in various shapes and forms in all but the very best work.

It was developed as a way to cover large areas with only small boards so that nothing would warp and allowance could be made for any shrinkage or expansion. Areas paneled were commonly around fireplaces and the lower portion of living room walls—which was referred to as wainscot.

"Wainscot" meant originally the wooden sides of a wain or wagon, and then referred to a type of imported (into England) Baltic or Russian oak, much used for this kind of work.

PLASTER
PLASTER GROUND
SMALL MOULDING
DADO CAP
TOP RAIL
FURRING STRIP
DADO PROPER
PANEL
BOTTOM RAIL
BASEBOARD
BASE SHOE

WAINSCOT

A much simpler form of wood paneling is the use of planks or small boards applied horizontally or vertically (or in any other direction if you will).

The boards may be simple square-edged plain boards, but for good work they are usually matched, that is, tongued and grooved and well-seasoned. If you are using square-edged boards and some shrinking is possible (using green rough-sawn lumber is very inexpensive and popular in some areas, and this shrinks a lot), put up black building paper or felt before you fix the boards. This doesn't stop the shrinking, but it makes the subsequent cracks less obvious.

VERTICAL PANELING

BUILDING PAPER (STAPLED TO STUDS)

The most important thing with this kind of paneling is to ensure that you have adequate nailing surfaces—before you start!

When paneling over masonary, such as concrete blocks, fix furring strips to the wall, using masonry nails.

As with all other types of wall covering, do not forget to apply a vapor barrier first, such as a sheet of plastic.

When working with tongued and grooved material, blind nail through the tongues for best appearances, as shown below.

Do not try to hammer the nail all the way in; you will only mar the wood; use a nail set. Similarly, use a nail set when face nailing square-edged material.

Another way to disguise cracks caused by the wood shrinking as it dries out is to use V-gooved T & G (tongued and grooved) wood. Knotty pine is most common in this form; for closets and bathrooms, smaller T & G boards of cedar, which is very aromatic, are available.

4. PLYWOOD PANELING

Plywood paneling, despite its imitative nature and relatively high cost per sheet, has become enormously popular with economy-minded builders, mainly because of the ease of application and consequent labor-saving.

Under the general heading of plywood paneling, I mean to include all kinds of plywoods, hardboards, and particleboards, all of which are available in a wide variety of thicknesses, textures, and patterns, but all of which usually are supplied in sheets measuring 4' x 8' (1.22 m x 2.43 m), making application virtually the same regardless of type.

Order what you need delivered a week or so before using it and a week or so after any sheetrocking has been completed to allow the paneling to acclimatize to the house's moisture condition and the sheetrock to cure properly (this also produces a lot of moisture). Store the panels flat. Choose matching nails, preferably finish nails that can be set in the paneling grooves and blended in.

The most important point is to have adequate nailing surfaces before you start. The sheets, being 4' x 8' (1.22 m x 2.43 m), if applied vertically (as is usual), should have joints aligned with the studs, which are usually 16" (406 mm) on center. However, because of doors and windows and other individual circumstances, the sheets will rarely line up with the studs. The solution is to install horizontal blocking every 4' (1.22 m) between the studs.

Unlike sheetrock, you can't hide chipped edges or corners, so be *very* careful. Try standing all the sheets up against the wall in the places they will go to check the resultant color matches and grain effects. Then start in one corner and work out.

Regardless of the wall, fix your panels perfectly plumb!

This will determine whether the room looks all right or not. Since most walls and ceilings do tend to vary a little (at least) from perfect plumb and perfect level, fix the first sheet with a small gap at the top (say 1/8" (3 mm)) between it and the ceiling, and this will hopefully take care of any minor ceiling irregularities.

Most rooms are around 8' (2.43 m) high. When paneling rooms which are just a little higher, it is often easiest to panel down from the ceiling and hide the difference at the bottom with base board (called skirting in Britain).

When you come to electric outlets and switches, measure carefully—as with sheetrock. Drill a small hole to start the cut out, then use a keyhole saw or small electric jigsaw. A good method for getting the hole in the right place is to measure down from the ceiling and across from the next panel.

Avoid denting the panel when nailing. It is better to set the nail with a nail set. Nail at the top first—this way it is easier to adjust the sheet.

Try to arrange the panels so they join over an opening as illustrated opposite; it is easier this way than having to cut the entire opening out of one panel.

THIS IS EASIER TO DEAL WITH THAN THIS

Leave all trim, such as ceiling moulding, door casing, etc., until all the paneling is up and all nails have been set.

Lastly, be very careful when moving the panels; watch all edges and corners all the time!

SPECIAL "T" MADE FROM SPARE STUD TO HOLD PANEL TO CEILING WHILE —NAILING—

WEDGE THIS END ON THE FLOOR

5. TILED AND SUSPENDED CEILINGS

Ceiling tiles are manufactured in a variety of designs and standards, some mainly for easy application and others for sound-deadening and noise-reduction.

The easiest application is with the use of furring strips nailed to the rafters or joists of the floor above. For **12" x 12" (305 mm x 305 mm)** ceiling tiles, simply nailing furring strips on **12" (305 mm)** centers and either nail, glue or, best of all, staple the tiles to the furring strips.

Arrange the furring strips so that the tiles lie symmetrically on the ceiling, having reduced tiles equal at both edges rather than at one side only.

The tiles may usually be cut with a utility or sheetrock knife. The edges of the ceiling may be supported by a ceiling moulding, so don't worry about furring stips where the ceiling meets the wall.

CEILING MOULDING

Suspended ceilings have the added advantage of being able to include flush lighting panels, making so-called luminous ceilings. Once again, there are numerous manufacturers, all with their own systems, but the basic procedure is similar in all cases.

Firstly, make an accurate plan of the ceiling to determine where the suspended runners which hold the panels (and sometimes joists directly above) will go. Normally these runners run parallel to the length of the room 2' (610 mm) apart and at right angles to the ceiling joists.

Then plan the position of the cross-members, which are usually 2' (610 mm) to 4' (1220 mm) apart. With the basic grid to include lighting panels in the ceiling.

Now run whatever wiring is needed, install the lighting fixtures, if these are not to be suspended with the ceiling, and make sure that the ceiling provides nailing for the hangers which hold the runners by nailing blocks between the joists if necessary.

Next fix the wall angles so they are level and at the right height.

Then attach hanger wires to the joists (and blocks) and attach the main runners, after which the cross-tees are snapped in.

Finally, lay in the ceiling panels and lighting modules, and the system is complete.

The actual suspension units may vary from manufacturer to manufacturer, but basically they are all similar to the units shown below.

WALL ANGLE

MAIN RUNNER

CROSS-TEE

CHAPTER FOUR
FLOORS

There are numerous kinds of floors designed for various requirements, but they may be generally classified as either:

1. SINGLE LAYER FLOORS or
2. DOUBLE LAYER FLOORS,

and with respect to the form of joint, in the case of wood strip floors, as:

1. STRAIGHT OR BUTT or
2. TONGUE AND GROOVE.

Special feature floors, such as soundproof or fireproof floors, are not covered here, since we are dealing with a basically simple owner-built residence where "special features" are less likely to be required.

SINGLE FLOORS

In cheaper construction, a single finish board often suffices, especially where there is a cellar heated by a furnace to keep the cold and dampness out.

There are also other instances where a single layer floor is adequate, such as in the basement itself or in workrooms. In any case, with a single layer floor, it is imperative that all joints be over joists.

Carefully sorting the boards to length before starting to lay them can often save much waste and also allows control over possible unwanted contrasts in grain and color between adjoining boards.

Another form of single layer floor is a plywood floor subsequently covered with linoleum, tile, or carpet. This is both quick and cheap in terms of labor, but ultimately not as long-lasting or as versatile as a finish wood floor, although it doesn't matter if the carpet is replaced whenever it wears out.

DOUBLE FLOORS

Usually the floor consists of two layers:

1. THE ROUGH OR SUBFLOOR
2. THE FINISH FLOOR

Subfloors, which were formerly made of rough boards laid diagonally across the joists or of matched boards laid at right angles to the joists, are now most commonly made of plywood laid down in 4' x 8' (1.22 m x 2.43 m) sheets.

The reason for laying the strip subfloor diagonally is to afford extra bracing, and because a finish floor is never laid in the same direction as a subfloor; but since the direction of a finish floor may change from room to room, diagonal subflooring is the only way to ensure a cross-laid pattern between subfloor and finish floor.

DIAGONAL
SUBFLOOR-
ING

PLYWOOD
SUBFLOOR

One constructional advantage of double floors is that the sub-floor being laid early on, often before the framing of the walls is begun (though sometimes after), a floor for the builder to walk on is provided which will take rough usage, the finish floor, not being laid until after the painting and all other heavy work is finished, being thus protected.

In any event, the construction of subfloors is fully covered in my earlier book, "**Illustrated Housebuilding**"; we are concerned here only with the finished aspects of flooring. Nevertheless, something which will pay dividends in securing a firm and squeak-free floor is to go carefully over the subfloor before laying the finish floor and make sure that it is flat, level, and well nailed. Squeaks occur because boards are not tight and consequently rub against one another. So if in doubt nail some more to make certain that every board is secure.

BEECH LEAVES

Between the subfloor and finish floor you should install a layer of **15** lb. building paper or deadening felt which stops dust and helps deaden the sound, and also, where the floor is over a basement or crawl space, will increase the warmth of the floor by preventing air infiltration.

FINISH FLOOR

BUILDING PAPER

SUBFLOOR

JOISTS

When you have laid the paper (which is black) it will be found very helpful to chalk in the location of the joists so you know where to nail the finish floor.

BUILDING PAPER

CHALK MARKS OVER JOISTS

The finish floor may consist of hardwoods or softwoods laid in various ways.

Softwood floors and strip flooring in general are usually laid crosswise to the joists and lengthwise to the room for best appearances. The softwoods now most commonly used are Douglas fir, redwood, Western larch, and hemlock and white pine.

The commonest hardwoods are oak and maple, although where expense is not a limiting factor birch, yellow pine, walnut, red gum, cherry, or mahogany can also be used (as may be the many other exotic and expensive hardwoods).

Hardwoods, when used in strips or boards, are similarly usually laid crosswise to the joists, but when used in short lengths, may be laid in various patterns, as in parquet.

RANDOM
WIDTH
FLOOR OF
PINE
BOARDS

PATTERNED FLOOR OF OAK & CHERRY (BARLBY CASTLE, KENT)

Before the twentieth century, square-edged single floor boards were the rule. Thickness varied, but was generally greater than is used today. Also, the widths were usually much greater too, sometimes up to as much as 36" (915 mm).

SQUARE-EDGED

The boards were face-nailed or pegged with hardwood pegs. Later the boards were rabbeted, and gradually tongued and grooved boards became the rule.

RABBETED

TONGUED &
GROOVED

Nowadays, when wide boards are used, screws are often set deep in the wood and the holes filled with circular wooden plugs.

The very best floor would be made of seasoned quarter-sawn hardwood, end-matched (this means every board is tongued and grooved on the ends as well as the sides), and hollow-sawn on the back to ensure firmer contact with the subfloor, since there is less surface which can be affected by any subfloor unevenness.

QUARTER-SAWN END-MATCHED OAK

HOLLOW-SAWN

It should be borne in mind, however, that with regard to how the board is sawn from the tree, plain-sawn, being cheaper because it is an easier cut, is more common than quarter-sawn.

PLAIN-SAWN

The boards are all sliced from the tree in one plane; consequently, the grain runs across the width of the board, making it easier to warp.

QUARTER-SAWN

All the boards are sawn from the center to the outside; thus the grain always runs at right angles, making the board more stable in shrinkage.

Softwood flooring is usually not end-matched and is usually wider—up to 8" or 10" (203 mm or 254 mm) is common—whereas hardwood flooring is more usual in widths from 1½" to 4" (38 mm to 107 mm), and also in shorter lengths.

The best way to obtain softwoods is to have a sawmill tongue and groove native wood, and mill one side only. This gives you a thicker board than one milled on both sides and is a lot cheaper. However, you will have to season it yourself; whereas hardwood flooring may be obtained in prefinished bundles which are supposed to be kiln-dried to the correct moisture content.

In any event, finish flooring should never be laid in a house which is damp, or which has been unheated during the winter months. Kiln-dried wood will quickly absorb moisture and swell, only to shrink again when dried out, leaving gaps between the joints.

GAPS CAUSED BY SHRINKAGE CAUSED BY FLOOR HAVING BEEN LAID WITH A TOO HIGH MOISTURE CONTENT

Storing the flooring in the house as long as possible before laying it (assuming the house is heated, if it is winter) is ideal. If you are laying softwood lumber obtained directly from the mill rather than the lumberyard, you should try and keep it at least six months before laying it.

LAYING A FINISH FLOOR

The first problem, having decided what kind of floor you are going to lay, is how much to order, because **100 sq. ft. (9.29 sq. m.)** of flooring does not cover **100 sq. ft. (9.29 sq. m.)** of floor area! This is because of the difference in actual and nominal measurements and because a certain amount of wood is invariably lost at joints and ends.

The smaller the units you are laying, the more you should add. For example, if you plan to floor a particular room, discover the area by multiplying the length of it by the breadth of it and add **25%** if the flooring is to consist of **2" (50 mm)** wide boards, or **33%** if it is to consist of **1½" (38 mm)** boards. This will give you enough if the room is rectangular—if there are bay windows, closets, or other nooks, add proportionally more.

2" (50mm) BOARDS:
LENGTH X BREADTH
+ 25%

1½" (38mm) BOARDS:
LENGTH X BREADTH
+ 33-1/3%

BREADTH

LENGTH

COMPUTING AMOUNT OF FLOORING NEEDED

As stated before, make sure the subfloor is level and tight. Do some extra nailing if necessary and see that all nails are well set. Lay down a good quality building paper.

Choose the right nails for the floor you are laying. For example, 25/32" (20 mm) thick matched tongue and groove flooring is best blind-nailed with 8d wire nails or cut flooring nails.

WIRE NAIL   CUT NAIL

For ½" (12 mm) thick flooring, 6d nails may be used.

Cut nails are better for use with hardwoods, since they punch rather than spread the fibers and are thus less likely to split the wood. Predrill whenever you think there is any danger of splitting—it only takes a few moments to drill, and even though it may upset your rhythm, the split board could lie there for years!

The floor should be begun and finished ½" (12 mm) from the wall to allow for any expansion and thus prevent any bucking. This gap is hidden either by the baseboard or the baseboard shoe as shown opposite. Therefore the baseboard should ideally be removed before you start.

LEAVING A GAP AND CONCEALING IT

Also, before you start, remove any doorway thresholds.

The first strip, or board, is laid with the grooved edge facing the wall, and is face-nailed along that edge and blind-nailed through the grooved edge.

The tongue of one strip fits into the groove of the next strip, snugly but not too tightly or the floor could buckle under damp circumstances.

Make sure that the first strip is straight by sighting along it and from time to time, as you approach the opposite wall, measure the width of floor laid for variation.

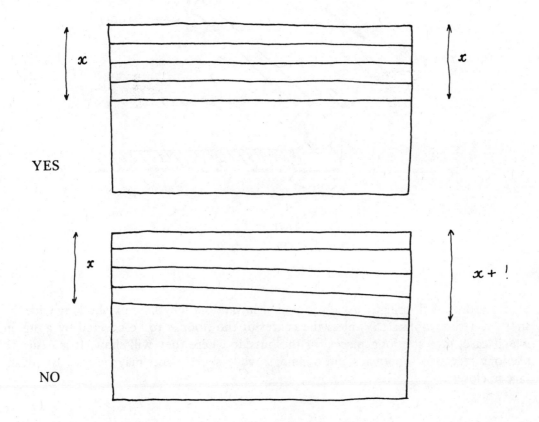

Nail to every joist, and when blind-nailing, do not strike the wood with the hammer or attempt to set the nail with the hammer alone; use a nail set.

Narrow width strip flooring may be laid three or four strips at a time and then driven tightly against one another.

Another method is to use a hammer gun, which fits against the tongue of the laid board and, being struck with a hard rubber mallet, drives a nail in at the right place and at the right angle. These guns may usually be rented from lumberyards where flooring is sold.

NAIL GUN

Since hardwood flooring is usually supplied in random lengths, mix the long with the short over the whole area—unless the center of the floor is to be covered by a rug, in which case, save the long pieces for the outside where they will show. It is easier to use long pieces for doorways and openings, while short pieces may be used to advantage in closets.

To drive the pieces tightly together, use a scrap piece of flooring and hit this rather than destroy the tongue of the strip being laid.

PIECE OF SCRAP

With wider boards, or longer bent pieces, the method is to nail a piece of scrap to the floor a little way ahead of the finish floor and drive a wedge in between, thus forcing the boards tightly together.

GAP

BLOCK NAILED TO FLOOR

WEDGE

HOW TO CLOSE GAP

All butt joints (the ends of the boards) should be staggered. This is equally important for both wide and narrow boards.

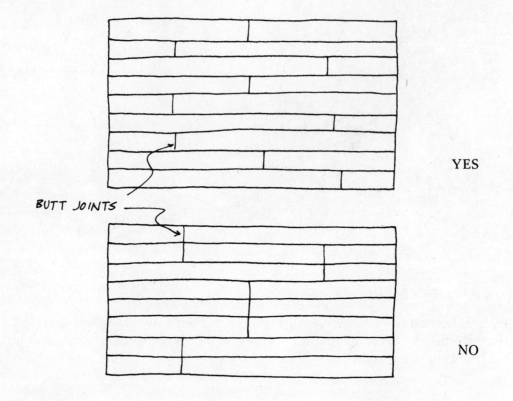

BUTT JOINTS

YES

NO

To lay boards in tight corners, and to lay the last few boards, fit them together as shown and press them into place by standing on them.

FITTING THE
LAST FEW
BOARDS

When all the floor is laid, replace all the trim, thresholds, and baseboards you may have removed.

When replacing the baseboard shoe, nail the shoe to the floor, not to the baseboard, or the baseboard, if it should shrink, might pull the shoe up from the floor and leave an unsightly gap.

YES

BASEBOARD

BASEBOARD SHOE
NAILED TO FLOOR

NO

BASEBOARD SHOE

BASEBOARD SHOE
NAILED TO BASEBOARD
AND FLOOR

The shoe is most conveniently made from "quarter-round." The actual baseboard may be anything from mill-made moulding or plain **1" x 2" (25 mm x 50 mm)** to an elegantly moulded skirting board up to **12" (304 mm)** high.

In all cases nail the baseboard to the studs. Cope the inside joints and miter the outside joints.

MILL-MADE   PLAIN STOCK

BASEBOARD TYPES   MOULDED

BUTT
JOINT

MITER
JOINT

COPED
JOINT

INSIDE CORNERS   OUTSIDE CORNERS

CHAPTER FIVE
STAIRS

The construction of stairs is, like the framing of roofs, one of the most difficult aspects of housebuilding, calling for the most amount of knowledge and the greatest degree of skill.

It is virtually an art in itself, since hardly any two staircases are exactly alike, each usually being built to accommodate a unique set of circumstances, each staircase thus presenting its own peculiar problems.

A whole volume could be written detailing the intricacies of stairbuilding, and yet the aspiring stair builder would still need much practical experience before he could call himself properly competent.

This section of this book does not therefore claim to be exhaustive, merely to present enough information so that the general principles may be grasped and thereby enable the builder to construct a straightforward staircase for a small residence.

If your situation demands a more complicated solution than is here provided and you do not intend to become a professional stair builder, then it would be better to contract the work and concentrate your energies elsewhere.

Nevertheless, there are sufficient opportunitites for relatively simple stair construction, such as stairs for porches, attics, basements, and sometimes even main stairs where the design is not too complicated, to warrant some discussion of stairbuilding.

Provided the theory and principles are thoroughly understood and careful workmanship is practiced, this work should not be beyond the builder or carpenter who has managed to construct the rest of the house.

More than any other aspect of housebuilding, stairbuilding has its own large vocabulary of terms which must be understood in order that the subsequent instructions may be followed. It is important therefore to familiarize yourself with the following definitions before proceeding further.

DEFINITIONS

STAIRS are a series of steps which afford communication between different levels.

STAIRCASE is the term properly applied to the space or enclosure occupied by the stairs and landings; although it is often used synonymously with "stairs."

A STEP is one of the footspaces or platforms in a flight of stairs. In wooden stairs the step usually consists of a RISER and a TREAD.

TWO STEPS WITH
TREADS & RISERS

Sometimes the riser is omitted.

FLYERS are steps in a flight of stairs that have rectangular treads and which are consequently parallel to each other as compared to WINDERS or TURN-STEPS, which are used in turning around a newel and which in consequence may have irregular or triangular treads, and which are not parallel to each other.

The outer end of the lowest step is often rounded, and is then known as a ROUND-ENDED or BULL-NOSE STEP; if the end is formed into a part of a spiral, it is known as a CURTAIL STEP.

OPEN STRING STAIR WITH BULL-NOSE STEPS

The NOSING or front edge of a tread may be SQUARE or ROUNDED or otherwise MOULDED. A straight edge laid on a flight of stairs to touch the nosings will give the LINE OF NOSINGS.

NOSING

STRING BOARDS, STRINGS, or STRINGERS, as they are now most usually called, are the sloping boards which hold the ends of the treads and the risers. In the illustration below, "a" is a section through a series of steps and shows one of the stringers in elevation; the treads and risers are housed in grooves cut in the stringer and held secure by wedges which are driven further in whenever the stairs begin to creak (because of the wood shrinking as it dries).

The inside angle formed by the tread and the riser is known as the SOFFIT ANGLE, and is supported by glued wedges as shown.

At "b" the same stringer is shown with the steps omitted.

CLOSE STRINGER

A stringer of the type shown opposite is known as a CLOSE STRINGER. In a flight of stairs with one string against a wall and the other exposed to view, the former is known as the WALL STRINGER and the latter as the OUTER STRINGER.

In contradistinction to the close stringer shown opposite, an OPEN or CUT STRINGER is cut away to receive the treads and risers. The riser and the stringer should be mitered together, the stringer therefore sometimes being known as a CUT AND MITERED STRINGER.

OPEN STRINGER

The nosing of the tread of an open stringer is "returned," that is, carried on around the end, as shown on the previous page. Older types of open stringers often had ornamental brackets fixed under the end nosings of the treads; the stringer was then said to be BRACKETED.

BRACKETED STRINGER

Stringers may be straight or curved; curved stringers are known as WREATHED STRINGERS.

A LANDING is the floor space at the head of a series of stairs. Such a series is known as a FLIGHT or a FLIGHT OF STAIRS. (A very descriptive and rather poetic term.)

When the stairs from one floor to another are divided into two flights, the stairs are said to be a PAIR OF STAIRS. If the upper flight is parallel to the lower flight, but rises in the opposite direction, a level floor the width of the two flights must be formed; this is known as a HALF-SPACE LANDING.

If the upper flight is at right angles to the lower, or if there are winders at the head of the lower flight or the foot of the upper flight, a landing half the size is sufficient, and this is called a QUARTER-SPACE LANDING.

The RUN or GOING of a flight of stairs is the horizontal distance from the FOOT or lowest riser to a point exactly below the HEAD or highest riser.

The RISE or HEIGHT is the vertical distance from floor to landing.

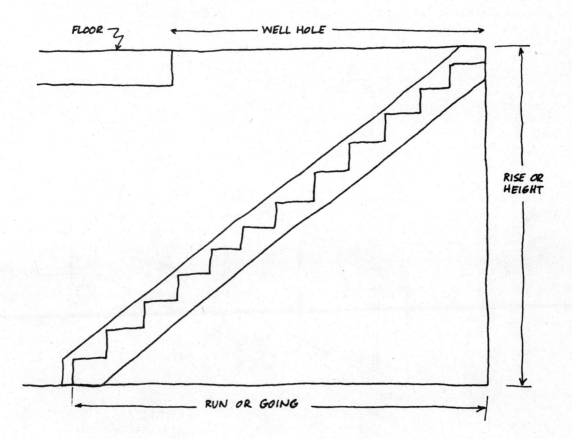

The WELL is the place occupied by a flight of stairs, and the WELL HOLE is the opening in the floor at the top of a flight of stairs.

NEWELS are posts receiving the ends of stringers and handrails, and are also pillars receiving the treads in a circular staircase. In more elaborate staircases, newel posts are the occasion for much turning and other decorative work, but they function as well if they are simple unadorned posts.

A DROP is the lower end of a newel that hangs down at the top of a flight of stairs.

BANISTER is the now more common form and corruption of BALUSTER, a word which was originally Italian, meaning "blossom of the wild pomegranate," the shape of which resembled the short pillar, circular in section, slender above and bulging below, used as one of a series to support the HANDRAIL, banisters and handrail together forming the BALUSTRADE.

HANDRAILS are plain or moulded rails fixed to the walls or newels for convenience and protection.

NEWELS &
BALUSTRADE

DOG-LEGGED STAIRS are those pairs of stairs where the outer stringer of the upper flight is directly over the outer stringer of the lower flight; both stringers are fixed into the same newel.

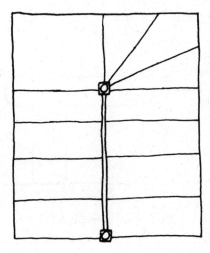

PLAN OF DOG-LEGGED STAIRS

GEOMETRICAL STAIRS have a space or well between the flights and no newel, the stringer being continued in a curve. In this case the stringer and the handrail are said to be WREATHED.

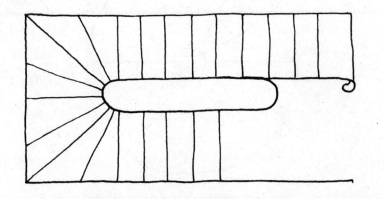

PLAN OF GEOMETRICAL STAIR

Strictly speaking, geometrical stairs not only wind around a central well, but have no half-space or quarter-space landings; stairs that do are properly called WELL STAIRS.

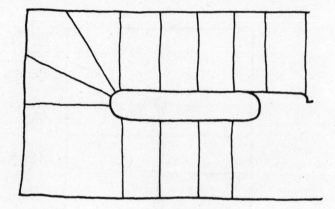

PLAN OF WELL STAIRS

CIRCULAR STAIRS have the treads and risers framed into a central post or newel around which the steps wind.

PLAN OF CIRCULAR STAIRS

Other more complicated forms of stairs are COCKLE STAIRS, which is a winding stair-case, a SPIRAL STAIRCASE in which all the steps are winders but revolve around a well, and ELLIPTIC STAIRS in which each tread converges so that in plan an elliptic ring is formed.

The CARRIAGE is the framework, including the stringers, which supports the steps.

BEARERS are supports for winders wedged into the walls and secured by the stringers.

TRIMMERS are the beams to which stringers are fixed at the top of one stair and the start of the next.

Where possible, stairs are considered best made with a right-hand wheel rather than left-hand, but it should be remembered that the form of stair can be worked out better in new buildings than in old buildings being remodeled.

SIMPLE STAIRS

Before proceeding to the complexities of orthodox stairbuilding, some simpler methods are here described which may be found useful for porch or attic steps, or for temporary purposes.

Next to the common ladder, the simplest kind of stair is a thick plank placed at a convenient slope to form the ascent, with pieces of wood nailed to it to give a firm footing.

PLANK STAIRCASE

PLANK

PIECES OF WOOD (NOT NECESSARILY TRIANGULAR) NAILED TO PLANK

SOLID OAK LOG STAIRCASE

This kind of staircase, made from solid oak logs of triangular section, pinned to two stout runners, was a common English construction for cellar stairs in the seventeenth century.

PINS

OAK LOGS

Another form of simple stair which is of interest because of its antiquity is shown below. While it doesn't require much accuracy or skill, there is, however, a considerable amount of labor involved.

STRINGERS

RISER , RESTS ON
TREAD, WHICH RESTS
ON SUPPORTS

OLD BRACKET
STAIRCASE

CROSS-SECTION

TREAD
RISER

SUPPORT

STRINGER

The stair next in degree of complexity to the plank stair is one composed of boards forming treads wide enough to provide a secure footing, fixed to two raking boards forming the stringers.

LADDER
STAIRCASE

The treads may be nailed directly to the stringers; this is the quickest and poorest solution.

NAILED

A better method than simply nailing through the stringers into the ends of the treads is to house the treads into the stringers, and then nail or screw.

HOUSED

Even better in terms of secureness, though perhaps not so neat in appearance, is the use of cleats. These are small strips fixed to the inside of the stringers; they may be nailed or screwed, though screws are stronger. To these are similarly nailed or screwed the treads. This system is perhaps easier than rabbeting out stringers for housing joints and affords greater lateral strength.

CLEATED

Yet another method of constructing ladder stairs is to mortise the treads into the stringers. The mortises are sometimes rectangular, as at "a," and sometimes for a nicer effect the mortises may follow the slope of the stringers, as at "b." For "mission style" staircases the tenons are carried right through the stringers and secured by keys, as at "c."

a

RECTANGULAR MORTISED LADDER STAIRCASE

INCLINED MORTISED LADDER STAIRCASE

b

c

MISSION STYLE LADDER STAIRCASE

The stringers are sometimes bound together by rods which are secured on the outside faces with washers and nuts. Such rods should be placed near the middle of a step, and close to its under side.

DOUBLE-STEP
STAIRCASE

For use where the ascent would be too steep for a regular stair.

PROPORTIONS

The two most important aspects of good stair design are that there be sufficient head-room and that the stairs be comfortable to ascend and descend. This last is governed by the proportions of the treads to the risers.

It is a general maxim that the greater the breadth of a step the less should be the height of the riser; and conversely, the less the breadth, the greater should be the height.

Experience shows that a step with a tread of 12" and a riser of 5½" may be used as a comfortable standard. Therefore, by using the following formula, we may determine the breadth of the tread if we know the riser, or the height of the riser if we know the tread:

Let **T** be the tread and **R** the riser of any step which has the proper proportions; then to find the proportion of any other treat **t** and riser **r**:

$$\frac{R \times T}{r} = t,$$

or

$$\frac{T \times R}{t} = r$$

For example, taking a tread of 12" and a riser of 5½" as the standard, then, to find the breadth of the tread when the given riser is 8", and substituting these values for **t** and **r** in the formula, we have:

$$\frac{12 \times 5½}{8} = 8¼ \text{ inches as the breadth of the tread.}$$

Another example, to find the height of the riser when the breadth of the tread is known to be **13"**:

$$\frac{T \times R}{t} = r$$

$$\frac{12 \times 5\frac{1}{2}}{13} = 5\ 1/13"\quad \text{as the height of the riser.}$$

This proportional variation between tread and riser may also be illustrated graphically, which can be useful if you want to make any drawings before you start to build (which often helps).

Firstly, substituting, for the sake of working with whole numbers, the dimensions in so many half inches, and accepting again the comfortable proportion of **12 to 5½**, draw a right-angled triangle with a base of **24** and a perpendicular of **11**.

24 (12")   11 (5½")

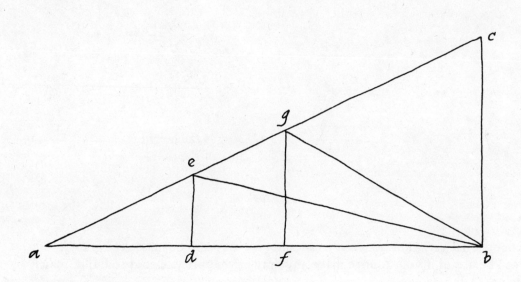

In this right-angled triangle, which we shall call a b c, ab equals 24 and bc equals 11.

To find the riser corresponding to a given tread, from b set off on **ab** the length of the tread, which we shall call **bd**.

Through **d** draw the perpendicular **de**, meeting the hypotenuse in **e**; then **de** is the height of the riser, and if we join **be**, we get the slope of the ascent.

Similarly, where **bf** is the width of the tread, **fg** is the riser and **bg** the slope of the stair.

Another method is by use of the following table, which, once again, accepts as the standard the proportions of **12" to 5½"** and extends the treads in inches and the risers in half inches.

It can be easily seen that these treads and risers will suitably pair together.

TREADS IN INCHES	RISERS IN INCHES
6	8½
7	8
8	7½
9	7
10	6½
11	6
12	5½
13	5
14	4½
15	4
16	3½
17	3
18	2½
19	2

Another very useful rule may be expressed as follows:

WIDTH OF TREAD + TWICE THE HEIGHT OF RISER = **24**, or:

$$T + 2R = 24$$

Transposing this we get: $T = 24 - 2R$, and $R = 12 - \dfrac{T}{2}$

Here are two examples showing the application of this rule:

First, let the riser be 7", then T = 24 - (2 x 7) = 24 - 14 = 10".

Second, let the tread be 12", then $R = 12 - \dfrac{T}{2} = 12 - 6 = 6$".

To avoid confusion the above examples have been expressed entirely in inches, but they work equally well if transposed into the metric system. To arrive at millimeters from inches, multiply the inches by **25.4000508**.

Since such multiplication can prove tiresome (if not inaccurate and productive of unhandy results), the following metric methods may be used instead.

Based on the assumption that the average length of a step is **600 mm** and that it is twice as tiring to climb upward as it is to walk forward, use the following formulae to obtain a comfortable riser and tread:

1. ONE TREAD + TWO RISERS = 600 to 620 mm.

Example: tread 250 mm + twice riser = 610 mm
twice riser = 610 - 250 = 360 mm

$$\text{riser} = \frac{36}{2} = 180 \text{ mm}$$

2. RISER X TREAD = 450

Example: tread 250 mm x riser = 450

$$\text{riser} = \frac{450}{250} = 180 \text{ mm}$$

Despite all of the above, however, it is seldom that the proportion of the tread and the riser is a matter of choice; the room allotted to the stairs usually determines this proportion; but the above rules will be found useful as guidelines, which you should try to approximate.

LAYING OUT STAIRS

Although the design of stairs is properly the work of an architect, the carpenter is often the one who has to do the final figuring out. This is actually the most difficult part and must be done most carefully or disaster will ensue. Once all the measurements have been correctly ascertained, the actual woodwork is not very difficult.

The most common situation the carpenter faces is having to build stairs in an already given space. If the stairs could be made to perfect proportions and then fixed in place with no obstructions, there would be few problems. However, the run or going is often predetermined and the problem is to figure the slope and size and number of the steps.

The proportions of tread to riser have been discussed in the previous section. The other important consideration when figuring stair layout is headroom.

Since the given dimensions are variable, *i.e.*, the opening in the second floor may be fixed, the available run may be fixed, the problem may be solved from different directions; but an example from one direction should suffice to explain the principles, and the variables may then be substituted as the situation dictates.

Let us therefore assume the distance between floors, *i.e.*, the rise for a straight flight of stairs to be "**x**," and the opening on the second floor to be "**y**."

The first step is to draw two lines representing the two floors. Call these two lines **ab** and **cd**, as shown over.

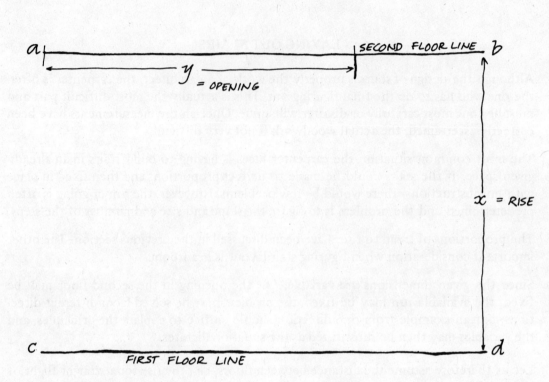

Now measure down from the second floor line to the ceiling underneath it—this will include the thickness of the finish floor, the subfloor if any, the joists, and the finished ceiling.

Call this measurement ef and mark it on your plan.

Now draw a vertical line down from **f** to represent the amount of headroom required to **g**

Next draw a line from **a** (the forward edge of the second floor opening) through **g** to meet the first floor line **ab**. Call the point where this line meets **ab** "**i**." The line **ai** is the angle of ascent and **ci** is the run or going.

The amount of headroom depends on what is convenient. If you make it about 7" (2.13 mm) it will sufficiently accommodate most human beings—except for giants, and they are usually accustomed to bending in buildings anyway.

You now know the rise (let us assume 9' (2.74 mm)) and the run. The next step is to find out how many steps will fit in this staircase.

Take as an average a riser of 7" and a tread of 10". (Remember the formula: 2 x RISER + TREAD @24; 2 x 7 + 10 = 24.) Simply divide the total rise of 9' by the height of an average riser of 7'. The answer is:

$$(9 \times 12) \text{ (to convert to inches)} \div 7 = 15.4$$

Since all risers must be the same size in any one staircase or you will trip over the odd one, we cannot have any fractions, so assume the number of risers to be 15.

There are two ways to discover the actual measurement of a riser now. Either divide the total rise by the number of risers:

$$(9 \times 12) \div 15 = 7.2", \text{ or}$$

take a story pole (a long straight stick) and, setting the dividers at a little over 7", step off the 9' distance representing the total rise. If there is a remainder, adjust the dividers until the 9' is exactly divided into 15 parts. Measure one of these parts and that is the measurement of a riser.

Now measure the total run as found in the diagram on the previous page as c_i. Let us assume that this works out to be 11'4½". Bearing in mind that the number of treads equals the number of risers minus one, as shown on the next page, we can work out the measurement of a tread by using the following formula.

$$\text{TREAD} = \text{RUN} \div \text{NUMBER OF STEPS}$$

$$\text{TREAD} = 11' 4½" \div (15 - 1)$$

$$\text{TREAD} = 136.5 \div 14 = 9.75"$$

FLOOR

4TH RISER

3RD RISER

3RD TREAD

2ND RISER

2ND TREAD

1ST RISER

1ST TREAD

FLOOR

4 RISERS

3 TREADS

SHOWING NUMBER OF TREADS EQUALS
NUMBER OF RISERS MINUS ONE

Now that you know the actual measurements of the treads and risers, complete the drawing as shown below.

x (RISE)

RISER = 7.2" or   1/15th of ac (x)

TREAD = 9.75" or

1/14th of ci

RUN

Note that the line of nosings, if you were to draw it in, does not coincide with the previously drawn angle of ascent.

There are two ways to complete the drawing on the previous page: one is to measure up from i 7.2" vertically, and then measure in horizontally 9.75" until you reach the top; or, more easily, divide x into 15 parts and draw a series of horizontal lines across the plan, and then divide ci into 14 parts and draw a series of vertical lines to intersect the parallel lines. The intersections thus formed constitute the previously defined line of nosings.

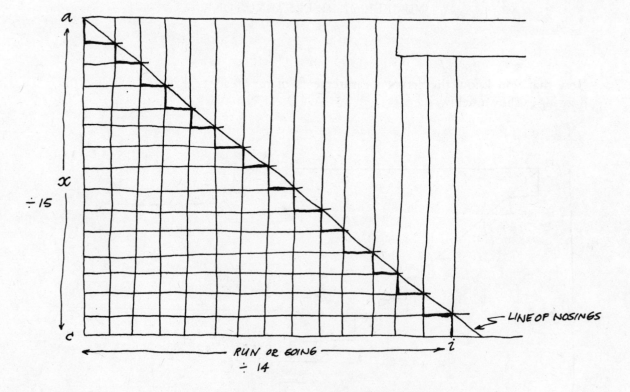

DRAWING IN THE
TREADS & RISERS

CUTTING THE STRINGERS

When the drawing has been completed and you have found all the pertinent dimensions, the next step is to make the stringers.

There are, as mentioned briefly before, three main types of stringers; open, close, and bracketed. The close stringer is and has been traditionally superior, since the treads and users can be wedged in place, and when shrunk and beginning to creak, can be made tight again by simply driving the wedges further in. To prevent open stringers from creaking is a little more difficult, but the construction is much simpler. However, the laying out of all three types is the same in principle, so we shall proceed with the easiest type as our example.

OPEN &
BRACKETED
STRINGER

CLOSE STRINGER

The open stringer may be marked for cutting out by the use of a carpenter's steel square (often made from aluminum to make it lighter), of a steel square with a fence attached, or by the use of a pitch board—this last being the most accurate of all three methods.

PLAN OF FENCE

PITCH BOARD

Using the steel square, as shown opposite is all right for common porch, attic, or basement stairs. For a little greater accuracy, make a fence out of a piece of straight hardwood, such as a piece of oak. Simply saw a slot down the middle and bore a few holes for nuts and bolts to clamp the fence tightly on the square. Wing nuts make any adjustment that may be necessary easy to make.

FENCE

The pitch board, which is cut to the exact measurements of the tread and riser, ensures even greater accuracy and only takes a few moments to make.

PITCH BOARD
IN USE

The most exact method, however, is to use a pair of dividers set to the step length or distance between nosings. This is found by calculating the distance along the face of the stringer and dividing it by as many steps as there will be.

This is a little difficult, since we have as yet no measurement for the finished overall length of the stringer. This can be seen by looking at the drawing below.

We have not calculated AB, nor do we have to. Since the riser height is known, simply lay off the second step a sufficient way along the board to leave room for the first step, and then, having thereby established the vertical angle of the riser, mark the first riser and draw a line at right angles back to the underside of the stringer.

By using the pitch board as many times as there are steps, the point B on the illustration opposite will ultimately be rreached. To check this, use Pythagoras' theorem which states that in any right-angled triangle the square of the hypotenuse equals the sum of the squares of the base and the perpendicular.

The run or going equals the base in the above theorem, and the total rise equals the perpendicular, both of which we know.

We need make only one adjustment to calculate the step length, and this is to subtract from the total rise the height of one riser, as shown below.

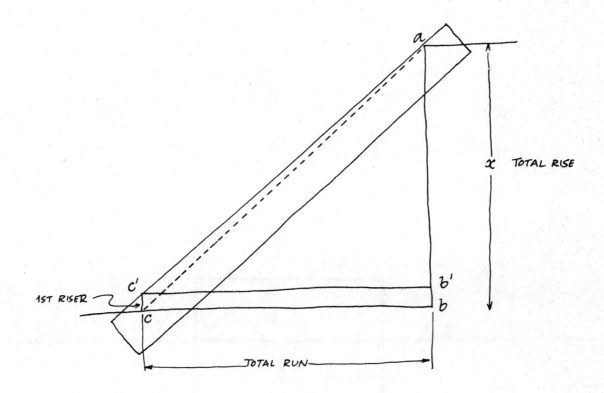

Transfer ab and ac from your previous working drawing (total rise and total run) and connect ac.

Erect a perpendicular at c to c', to equal the height of a riser. Now connect ac' which is the "step length" of the stringer. Draw c'b' parallel to cb.

In the triangle ab'c', $ac' = \sqrt{ab'2 + b'c'2}$

This is the length which must be stepped off by the dividers into as many steps as there are.

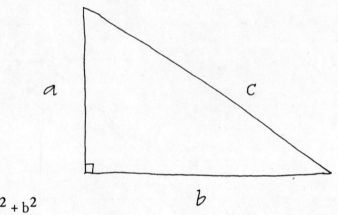

$$c^2 = a^2 + b^2$$

PYTHAGORAS' THEOREM

Depending on the wood used and its dimensions, stairs over a certain width may require a center stringer for extra support. If the outside stringers are open stringers, then you may use the waste portions to build up the center stringer as shown below.

BLOCKS CUT FROM
SIDE STRINGERS

NAILS

CENTER STRINGER

The best material is usually oak, since this is very hard weaving. At least full inch should be used, but five-quarter (31.5 mm) is better. If the stair is not to get much wear, such as a little-used basement stair, then of course some less expensive wood may be employed.

NEWELS

The only important requirement for the newel is that it be fixed very securely, since it holds the foot of the stringer and the handrail.

The actual design is capable of almost infinite variation, providing a square section to receive the end of the stringer and a square section to receive the end of the handrail is provided.

The stringer should be mortised into the newel as shown.

Securing the newel to the floor is all-important. Ideally, the newel should run down beneath the floor and be spiked to the side of a joist.

If this is not possible, try furring the joist out, or even cutting part of the newel away.

JOIST FURRED OUT AND BOLTED   NEWEL NOTCHED OVER JOIST

If the joists run the wrong way, or are too far away from the foot of the newel, make a pair of bridges as shown.

If none of the above is possible, bolt the newel to the floor, using a reinforcing block and mortising into the finish floor.

HANDRAILS

It is no exaggeration to say that as much could be written on the complexities of handrails as has been written in this entire book. But labor is more expensive today than it was formerly and the average handrail has become a far more straightforward affair.

It may be bought in lengths at any good lumberyard, often in a selection of mouldings, together with appropriate hardware (or ironmongery as it is called in Britain).

As stated in the introduction, this book is not meant to be an exhaustive treatise on all aspects of joinery, but a practical guide for the layman or beginner building a simple house.

However, if you have come this far, you will have a good foundation for more advanced joinery, should you so desire. There is a lot more to the subject, probably too much for any one person. As mentioned earlier, there are craftsmen totally occupied with but single aspects of this book. And, unless we all return to caves and trees, there will always be a need for this knowledge, from its simplest form to its most complicated.

SWAN-NECK AND MITER-CAP
AT THE TOP OF A RAIL

Finis